Gouldtown

A Very Remarkable Settlement of Ancient Date

Studies of some sturdy examples of the simple life, together with sketches of early colonial history of Cumberland County and southern New Jersey and some early genealogical records

By William Steward
and
Theophilus G. Steward

Published by Pantianos Classics

ISBN-13: 978-1-78987-554-6

First published in 1913

William Steward

Contents

Foreword vi

Chapter One - Gouldtown; its Tradition; its People; its General History 8

Chapter Two - Fenwick; English History; His Sailing and Landing; His Colony 14

Chapter Three - Fenwick Colony; Land Grants and Primary Government 23

Chapter Four - Copies of Very Ancient Parchment Deeds in Possession of a Bridgeton Attorney Deed 28

Chapter Five - Gould Traditions; Evidences; Descent; Benjamin Gould's Will 31

Chapter Six - The Early Goulds and Their Associations; the Pierces and Murrays; the Three Foundation Families 36

Chapter Seven - Origin of the Pierce, Murray, and Cuff Families 39

Chapter Eight - Importance of Genealogical Research; Some of the Original Family Genealogies of Salem and Cumberland Counties; Compilation of Thomas Shourds 42

Chapter Nine - Rural Sociological Examples, Suggested in this Life of Simplicity 50

Chapter Ten - Gould Genealogies; Probability of Origin of Name of the Settlement 55

Chapter Eleven - The Cuffs of Salem; Their Probable Origin; Their Ultimate Connection with the Gould, Pierce, and Murray Families. 72

Chapter Twelve - Genealogical Sketch of John Murray's and David Murray's Families and Some of the Pierce Connections 75

Chapter Thirteen - Family Eugenics and Longevity; the Gould, Pierce, and Murray Estates 85

Chapter Fourteen - Organization of the Church; Early Religious Affiliations of the People 89

Chapter Fifteen - The People's Patriotism; Ready to Bear Arms for the Country 98

Chapter Sixteen - Social Life; Some Typical Social Events; Two Golden Weddings; a Social Study 100

Chapter Seventeen - Educational Facilities of the Neighborhood. 111

Chapter Eighteen - Some Literary Efforts of Gouldtown Youth Thirty and Fifty Years Ago 119

Chapter Nineteen - A Story in Blank Verse 127

Chapter Twenty - Some Present Real Estate Possessions of the Inhabitants of Gouldtown 139

Foreword

It has long been in mind to prepare and put in book form the oral traditions, as well as such authenticated facts, as could be collected from records and public documents of the remarkable settlement of people of color, which has here been attempted.

The study of the three original families herein set forth in this county (Cumberland) and a fourth family connected to a degree with them, of Salem county origin, is a subject of some interest. That it is of more than local interest has been shown by lengthy newspaper articles in many metropolitan journals during the last thirty years.

The settlement was made the subject of historical allusion more than three-quarters of a century ago; and while many of those periodical articles have been based upon very insufficient information, the writers having been attracted to the subject by the historical allusions above referred to, they have been of a character indicating estimation.

To preserve these traditions, records, and histories as well as some of more enlarged interest, is the object here had in view.

W. and T. G. S.

The Village of Gouldtown. Sketched by 16-year-old Gouldtown Schoolgirl.

Chapter One - Gouldtown; its Tradition; its People; its General History

In Judge Lucius Q. C. Elmer's history of Cumberland County, New Jersey, written in 1865, occurs this statement:

"Gouldtown — partly in the Northern part of Fairfield, and partly in Bridgeton Townships — although never more than a settlement of mulattoes, principally bearing the names of Gould and Pierce, scattered over a considerable territory, is of quite ancient date. The tradition is that they are descendants of Fenwick."

Judge Elmer, a distinguished Supreme Court Jurist of New Jersey, was the son of General Ebenezer Elmer, who was an officer in the Revolutionary Army, first as an ensign, and shortly after as lieutenant in a company, and later, being a physician, serving as a surgeon; he served, in all, during the war of the Revolution, a period of seven years and eight months. In 1814, he commanded a brigade of militia called out for the defence of Philadelphia against the British, and was ever after that known as General Elmer. Judge Elmer was born soon after the close of the Revolution in 1793, and had ample opportunity and ability for research in his native county. He died in 1883.

Much interest has always been taken in the community of Gouldtown by the neighboring communities, and this was always of a friendly character; in early times because of its traditional descent, and later because of the ethnological features recognizable.

General Elmer and his son were accustomed, on Sunday afternoons to meet in a schoolhouse and catechize the children of Gouldtown, in the neighborhood, in the years following the Revolution. These children and youth would not all be mulattoes (the term "mulattoes" is used in this book in its general significance, applying to the people of color of mixed blood) however, for in the community were pure white families - as for instance the Woodruffs, the Luptons, the Fullers, the Seeleys, and the Whites, and others; traces of whom are to be found only in the farms they left, which were known by their names as the "Fuller Fields," the "White Fields," the "Jay Fields"; the names remaining a century or more after their owners had vanished. Only one of these names has been perpetuated in a village, and that of recent date and several miles distant from the original location. This is Woodruffs, about three or four miles northward from Gouldtown. It is a wealthy farming settlement on the line of the Central Railroad, and has a Methodist Church and a schoolhouse and post-office.

Gouldtown is comprised in two sections— following the two family names of Gould and Pierce, which were always known by their separate names, Gouldtown and Piercetown, but both known comprehensively as Gouldtown. It is remarkable in that it has perpetuated its family name in its locality for nearly two hundred years; also because it is a community of mulattoes who, contrary to the pet theory of some astute ethnological scientists, have perpetuated themselves generation after generation for almost two centuries; remarkable, too, for the known longevity of its people, who do not begin to grow old, as is often said, until they come to threescore years, and a number of whom have reached the century mark, one of whom (Ebenezer Pierce Bishop) is still living, at this writing, who is one hundred and six years old, and one of whom (Mrs. Lydia Gould Sheppard) was buried in the year nineteen hundred and eleven, at the age of one hundred and two, in the Gouldtown Cemetery, and a number of others who are still living at ages between seventy and ninety-five years.

Kellenberger's Pocket Gazetteer of New Jersey says; "Gouldtown — a post hamlet in Fairfield Township, Cumberland County, three miles southeast of Bridgeton, the county seat, which affords the nearest banking and shipping facilities, and is connected by daily stage (now by trolley cars). Here are two churches and a store. Population one hundred and fifty."

Formerly it had a post-office, but, since the opening of a trolley line, that has been abolished for lack of patronage, and its first postmaster, Seneca Bishop, whose mother was a Pierce, was, perhaps, the first colored postmaster in this country. At his death Mordecai C. Pierce was made postmaster; he was succeeded by his widow, Mrs. Anna Gould Pierce, at his death, and she held the position when the office was abolished.

The actual village is situated two and a half miles east from Bridgeton, the county seat of the County of Cumberland, but, as Judge Elmer states in his history, it is "scattered over a considerable territory," extending in a line of contiguous properties owned by the Goulds and Pierces and their connections from the farm of William C. Gould (inherited from his father, Furman Gould, Jr.), on East Avenue, Bridgeton, eastward to the farm of Stewart Haines Pierce near Carmel (inherited from his father, Adrian Pierce), a distance of almost seven miles; this long stretch of properties extends in width from one to three miles.

Several of the earlier Goulds and Pierces as well as Murrays intermarried with whites, and members of their immediate offspring went away and lost their identity, they and their descendants becoming white; while, from those who still maintained their identity as people of color, there have come many who have reached distinction, and in whom their native County shows merited pride, as, for instance, a Methodist bishop, a chaplain in the United States regular army, a physician, a lawyer, a distinguished dentist, teachers, writers, journalists; and in the industrial arts, carpenters, masons, blacksmiths, wheelwrights, painters, carriage builders, woolen spinners and weavers;

brickmakers, machinists, engineers, electricians, printers, factory men, sailors, ministers of the Gospel, and farmers; in fact none of its sister villages has produced — taking equality of environment — more or better or more creditable individualities than has this settlement.

Surrounding Bridgeton and from one to seven miles distant are the post towns and villages of Roadstown, Cohansey, Shiloh, Deerfield, Carll's Corner, Woodruffs, Fairton, Gouldtown and Bowentown, the two last having no post-offices.

The Bridgeton and Millville Traction Company's trolley line passes through Gouldtown, along the beautiful Bridgeton and Millville Turnpike; the distance between the two cities, Bridgeton and Millville, is ten miles, — Gouldtown two and a half miles from the former and seven and a half miles from the latter city, with hourly car traffic connection with each. The settlement is an ancient one, the inhabitants tracing their ancestry back to earliest colonial times.

The community possesses two churches situated about a mile apart, one a Methodist Episcopal, and the other an African Methodist Episcopal; the latter being in the village, the former in that part of the neighborhood now called Fordsville, the congregation of which is dominated by the Pierce family, while the Goulds are the dominating family in the African Methodist Episcopal Church.

This settlement, comprising all the families and both churches, is important for many reasons other than those before enumerated. That it does not abound in wealth and culture is due in great part to the fixed habits of the people and to the fact that they have been all these years domiciled upon poor, timber-exhausted lands. The same labor, economy, and thrift which they have practised here, employed in homes upon a more productive soil, would long ago have placed many of the industrious, sober, and self-denying families of Gouldtown in circumstances of substantial comfort, if not of affluence. They are not as slothful and backward farmers as one might presume from the neglected appearance of too many of their homes and their teams; but their poor land, coupled with the increased cost of living, compels them to give their attention to pressing necessities, to the neglect of the things which would add to appearances. They are interested in agriculture, close observers, and hard workers; and considering the conditions, obtain from their fields fair crops. They have estates ranging from $1000 to $15,000 or $20,000.

As far back as 1860, a large audience assembled to listen to a well-prepared paper on agriculture delivered in the Gouldtown schoolhouse by a young man of the neighborhood, who had not then reached his majority. In that paper he cited methods of cultivation practised in China; dealt with the pulverization of the surface; descanted upon the value of "compost," and spoke of utilizing mud and forest leaves as fertilizing agencies. A half century ago there was a Moral and Mental Improvement Society in Gouldtown, and it was from this society's library that the youth borrowed and read Dick's Works and by those books was inducted into the primary mysteries of natural philosophy. Many simple experiments were made by the boys of the community after the models given by that interesting writer. This library contained many volumes of standard works.

The "Saturday Evening Post" was regularly read by the principal families, as were also some of the early magazines. Such books as the History of England; Burns' Poems; Pilgrim's Progress; Robinson Crusoe; Josephus; Plutarch's Lives, Milton, and Shakespeare, were among those owned and read by the families. Perhaps few books were more highly prized by the devout than Baxter's "Saints' Rest"; but works of fiction were eagerly read and, we might say, studied, by many inhabitants of Gouldtown two and three generations ago. In my early childhood I heard the "Last Days of Pompeii" discussed by women of Gouldtown. Had they possessed the means and received the encouragement, several persons of the community would have made commendable progress in literature. Despite their surroundings, the generations that have passed away contained within them several who could be classed as well-read.

Lummis-Gouldtown School House

The principal institutions outside of the family were, and are still, the school and the church. Up to 1860 these both occupied the same building, the circuit preacher getting around once every three or four weeks. In the interval the pulpit was supplied by local preachers, among whom was "Uncle Furman Gould," the first preacher of any kind known among the Goulds. The preaching, both of the circuit preacher and of the local preacher, occupied itself exclusively with the eternal themes of "fleeing the wrath to come," and securing a home in heaven. The hardships of poverty, and homes on earth, had no place in their sermons. They had no lessons to give save such as might tend to make the "souls" of their hearers "prosper." The preachers as such had nothing to contribute to aid the people in making their homes more attractive and sanitary, or their farms more productive.

The same with even more emphasis could be said of the school. The Gouldtown school was a typical "Districk" school with its own Board of Trustees. These trustees, three in number, with very little knowledge of school books or methods, hired the schoolmaster who, without examination or license, started in on the appointed day to "keep school." These schoolmasters never had one word to say as to the purpose of education, and never related it, except in "ciphering," to anything in the actual lives of the scholars. They were taught to spell, to read, to write, and to cipher; but were taught nothing on life, conduct, and character - nothing that might aid or inspire youth to advance materially or even intellectually. The idea of the general improvement of the student did not seem to be present. It is painful to say, but nevertheless true, that neither the church nor the school as they existed in Gouldtown under the old methods contributed anything directly to the material or moral growth of the community. That the church contributed powerfully indirectly, by the stress it put upon conscious spiritual life, must be admitted; and that the school did the same by its almost mechanical methods of teaching children to read and write; but both failed to enter into, to improve or brighten, the every-day life of the people as they might have done. Nothing that either taught had the slightest bearing upon their most burning question. How to wring a living out of poor land? Their actual situation, crying as it was, called forth no sympathetic response from either church or school. The teachers were almost always white men, and, it must be said, did their best.

   Nevertheless, the people have held on to their land from generation to generation; have bought and cleared land; reared families and developed character. It must be said also that much of the land held by the Gouldtowners of to-day is of but little more exchangeable value than it was fifty years ago, though more productive now than it was then. Thus, instead of rising on a tide of general increase in the values of real estate, their fate, through no fault of their own, has been just the opposite. Instead of an unearned increment enhancing their holdings, there has fallen to them an unmerited decrement, taking from them as by the stealth of night the modest fortunes they had acquired. The changes in farming and living which have come over the country within recent years, and especially the development of market gardening, and market farming in the South with the cheap and abundant facilities for transportation, have very seriously affected the Jersey farmer. He has had to make the most thorough readjustment of both means and ends. In the early days the average Gouldtown farmer had but the one end in view, namely, to produce enough from his farm to furnish food for his family and provender for the stock that he kept. He managed usually to have tough horses, and fattened his hogs well; but his cattle were of the comparatively milkless wandering "breachy" variety that no one would have to-day. The corn, wheat and oats from his farm coupled with salt hay from the marsh, with potatoes, turnips and cabbage and a little clover hay; a few by-products, with a fair sowing of buckwheat and rye, furnished rations for man and beast and fattened the hogs from which an ample supply of well-cured hams, pork and lard was made, and, with many, a fatted beef was annually killed and salted down. In some cases, wool from their own sheep made their clothing, and rags from worn-out clothes were woven into the carpets that covered their floors.

Modernism has compelled the farmer of Gouldtown to adopt different aims, and to farm for the market, or rather for the middleman who stands in the market gate. In some cases he raises tomatoes and other articles to be delivered directly to the canners on contract, but often his goods go to the commission man for whose labor and skill the farmer pays on one end, and the consumer on the other. Entering the markets the Jerseyman finds himself, as has been previously intimated, in the presence of growers from the South; and their cheaper labor and earlier seasons, again call for readjustment of *methods* so that his goods may appeal to customers through their quality and appearance. It is to the credit of the Jersey farmer that it can be said he has weathered the storm and has not been crowded out of the markets. Jersey products and poultry hold the highest rank in our great Eastern markets.

The people of Gouldtown, especially the Goulds, have never been very ardent lovers of money; they have rather placed stress upon the development of the social and spiritual nature. Despite their very severe condition they have kept up from earliest times those customs of social enjoyment, indoors in winter and outdoors in summer, which have made them famous for generous hospitality. All the instruction which they received for generations both with regard to the work of their fields and the manner of entertaining guests, was that which came down from parent to child by oral tradition, until the coming in of modernism with its Farm and Home Journals and the like; yet they have maintained themselves well socially.

Bishop Benjamin F. Lee

Several years ago in the city of Washington an official from New Jersey in a public speech referred to the sterling character of individuals of Gouldtown and of their general good deportment. "I can remember well when a schoolboy there, that there was not a boy in school who swore; and I remember noting at one time there was not a child in school who could not read." [T. G. S.] Few inhabitants of Gouldtown proper, from earliest times, were actually illiterate, although none was highly educated. The following quotation from a recent Bridgeton paper will show in what light the community is regarded by its neighbors.

GOULDTOWN HONORED

There is no section of our County more highly honored than is Gouldtown, from which men have .gone forth to become widely known and honored.

Bishop Benjamin F. Lee was for some time, before he was made a Bishop, President of Wilberforce University at Wilberforce, Ohio, of which he is now a member of the Advisory Board. He is a man of solid piety, an able preacher and highly honored by all who know him, as well as by those of his own church.

Another is Theophilus G. Steward, who, for many years was chaplain of the United States Army and now since being on the retired list, ably fills a professorship at Wilberforce University. He is a preacher of far more than ordinary ability and able to acceptably fill any pulpit in the land.

Yet another is Theodore Gould, who is a member of the Philadelphia Conference of his church and for several years has acceptably filled the office of presiding elder. He also is a man of noted piety and of much ability as a preacher.

We doubt if there is another section of the County from which three more highly honored and useful men have gone forth.

Chapter Two - Fenwick; English History; His Sailing and Landing; His Colony

The restoration of the Stuart monarchy in 1660, was followed by the war with the Dutch during which the King, Charles II, granted to his brother James, Duke of York, all the lands the Dutch had held in America. The grant, as formally stated, included a large portion of the Province of Maine, and the country from the west side of the Connecticut River to the east side of Delaware Bay. This grant included Martha's Vineyard, Nantucket, all Long Island and the whole of the territory of New Netherland.

The next month after the grant was made a fleet of four ships, with a force of three or four hundred men, under the command of Colonel Richard Nicolls, as the lieutenant-governor of the Duke, sailed from England. With Nicolls were joined as commissioners Sir Robert Carr, Sir George Cartwright and Samuel Maverick, with extraordinary powers for settling all difficulties in the New England colonies, as well as to take possession of the Dutch province and reduce its inhabitants to obedience.

No sooner was the province fairly in English hands than new names were given to different portions, its boundaries were as far as possible defined, and grants of land were made to Englishmen. That region lying between the Hudson and the Delaware was named Albania, and grants and purchases were made within its boundaries from Sandy Hook to the mouth of the Raritan, and from the Raritan to the Achter Cul, now Newark Bay. But before Nicolls, in the name of the Duke of York, had taken possession of all New Netherland, the Duke, in anticipation of that event, granted in June, 1664, the whole country, from the Hudson to the Delaware and from latitude 41° 40' to Cape May, to two favorites of the Court, Lord Berkeley and Sir George Carteret.

To the new province of New Cesarea, the name of New Jersey was given, in commemoration of Carteret's defence of the Channel Island of Jersey against the forces of the Commonwealth in 1649.

Of this grant, however, Nicolls knew nothing till June, 1665, when Captain Philip Carteret arrived as Governor of the new province. There was, of course, no alternative but to receive with courtesy one coming armed with such credentials, though Nicolls represented to the Duke that he had hastily given away the fairest portion of his dominion.

A storm had driven Carteret's ship, the Philip, into Chesapeake Bay, but in July she arrived at New York, and a few days later anchored off the point now known as Elizabethport, New Jersey, and landed her thirty emigrants. At the head of these people, Carteret, with a hoe over his shoulder, marched to the spot he had chosen for a settlement, two or three miles inland, and to which in honor of the Lady Elizabeth, the wife of Sir George Carteret, he gave her name. He found at the point where he and his people landed, four families who had taken possession of lands under the grant which had been made by Nicolls. The newcomers brought with them the title of a new English province, and though more than one settlement had been earlier made by the Dutch on this side of the Bay of New York, this was the actual beginning of the State of New Jersey at Elizabeth.

Four years before, the West India Company had discerned and sought to take advantage of the discontent and apprehension felt by so many of the English, both at home and in the colonies, at the restoration of Charles II. The directors invited them to settle on the Raritan, or in its neighborhood, and offered them most favorable terms. Three of the magistrates of New Haven, where this discontent was very .general, Matthew Gilbert, the Deputy Governor, Benjamin Fenn, and Robert Treat entered into negotiation with Stuyvesant upon the subject, on behalf of some New Haven people, and found no difficulty in getting from the Dutch Governor the promise that a hearty welcome would be given and religious freedom be secured to any Puritan Colony that should plant itself within the Dutch jurisdiction. But the English asked also for political independence, and the negotiations were suspended. The question of civil relations Stuyvesant felt must be referred to his superiors at home.

Even that concession, he was instructed, the Directors were disposed to make to almost any, provided that Dutch supremacy was acknowledged in the last appeal. The New Haven people were the most eager to set up anew for themselves when the Winthrop charter brought them within the jurisdiction of Connecticut, and they would, perhaps, had there been time enough, have yielded somewhat in their demands. But while diplomacy hesitated events made no halt. Before any agreement could be reached satisfactory to both parties, New Netherland ceased to be a Dutch colony, and the Duke of York had granted to its new proprietors the whole region from the Hudson to the Delaware. [1]

The land granted by the Duke of York to Berkeley was soon after sold by him to John Fenwick, who in turn was obliged to part with nine-tenths of it to William Penn, Gauen Laurie, and Nicholas Lucas, to satisfy certain serious obligations, leaving for himself but one-tenth, or "ten-hundredths," as it was called. This John Fenwick was the second son of Sir William Fenwick, Baronet of Northumberland, and had already attained a degree of celebrity. The story of his life as related by John Clements is as follows:

He was second son of Sir William Fenwick, Baronet, who represented the County of Northumberland in the last Parliament under the Commonwealth (1659), and one of four brothers, Edward, John, Roger and Ralph. In 1640 Sir William had his residence at Stanton Hill, of Stanton Manor, in the parish of Horsely, Cumberland, where he had considerable landed estate. The mother, Elizabeth, was perhaps of one of the border families, and brought to her husband additional property, increasing his wealth and influence. John was born in 1618, at Stanton Hall, but the day of the month is not known. In 1636 he was styled Knight and Baronet, and five years after that time he married Elizabeth, daughter of Sir Walter Covert, Knight of Slaughan, Sussex. This lady was mother of his children, and from her came the direct and collateral branches in New Jersey. The family was of Saxon origin, and formed a powerful clan in Northumberland. Their ancient fastness was in the fenny lands about Standfordham, a small town near the Southern boundary of the shire before named.

The tower of Fenwick at Widdington, in Northumberland, near the coast of the North Sea, shows its antiquity in its rude strength and scanty limits similar to those built by the Saxon invaders during the fifth and sixth centuries. This was probably the first seat of the family after their coming over, and whence it may be traced through many of the shires of England.

In the ninth year of the reign of Edward III (1334) an inquisition was had of New Castle, and Johannes Fenwick was twice appointed Sheriff. During that time it was much enlarged and strengthened, being an important point of protection and defence against the Scotch. In those warlike times this place had no commercial importance, but had grown to be one of the largest ports in England.

The enmities of former generations have passed away, and what was once a necessary appendage to every town is now visited by the curious to see the means of defence in a barbarous age. In the twelfth century, Sir Robert Fenwick of Northumberland endowed the Abbey of New Minster, in the same shire, with two parts of his villa of Irdington, in Cumberland, thus showing his liberality towards, and his adherence to, the Catholic Church.

John Fenwick having passed through his law studies at Gray's Inn, London (1640), abandoned his profession for a season and accepted an appointment in the Parliamentary Army. His first commission reads as follows:

You are hereby ordered and required as Major under Colonel Thomas Barwis in his regiment of cavalry which was raised in the County of Westmoreland to assist the garrison of Carlisle, and to exercise the officers and soldiers under his command according to the discipline of war. And they are hereby required to yield obedience unto you as Major of said regiment. And all this you are authorized unto, until the pleasure of the Parliament of the Lord General be known.

Given under my hand and seal at Bernard Castle, 27th day of October, 1640.
To John Fenwick, Major, These. O. Cromwell.

In the same year he was ordered by the Parliament, with horse and dragoon to relieve Holy Island Castle in Durham. It was besieged by the royal troops and well nigh captured, when he appeared and defeated the enemy. He was an active and efficient officer, having the confidence of the Parliament and the Protector. After the trial and sentence of the King, he was detailed as commander of cavalry, in conjunction with the foot troops under Colonel Hacker, Colonel Hanks, and Lieutenant-Colonel Phayor, to attend the execution.

The order ran in this wise:

These are therefore to will and require you to see the said sentence executed in the open streets before Whitehall, upon the morrow, being the thirtieth of this instant, month of January, between the hours of ten in the morning and five in the afternoon of the same day, with full effect. And these are to require all officers and soldiers and others the good people of this nation of England to be assisting unto you in this service.

Given under our hands and seals, etc., etc.

This warrant was signed by all the members who sat as judges upon his trial, and the most of whom witnessed the carrying out the sentence. In the discharge of this important and delicate duty the most reliable officers and the best disciplined troops were selected, which placed John Fenwick among the first of those in the army about London at that time.

The religious status of John Fenwick during this period is doubtful and contradictory. While he was with the army he became a convert to the opinions of George Fox, and by a certificate dated February 11, 1649, he is shown to have been a member of the Independents, a denomination of Christians more Presbyterian than Quaker. Be that as it may, he eventually adopted the principles and practices of Friends and adhered to them until his death. The narrative goes on to recite what has already been stated as follows:

After the restoration, Charles II granted to his brother, James, Duke of York, "All that main land with several islands near New England called New Cesarea or

New Jersey in America" and James granted the same lands and premises unto John Lord Berkeley, Baron of Stratton, and Sir George Carteret, Knight and Baronet. Berkeley soon after sold his half of the lands to John Fenwick, and Fenwick, as has been said, was obliged to part with ninety one-hundredths of this land to William Penn, Gauen Laurie, and Nicholas Lucas, keeping to himself but ten-hundredths of the original purchase. After having relieved himself from his pressing debts he set out to occupy these possessions.

There was a want of unity in his family, growing out of a second marriage, and so deep rooted was it that his wife was not willing to go with him beyond the sea. His daughters, not realizing the perils incident to the settlement in a new country, but filled with the spirit of adventure and buoyant with the prospect of a change, required no persuasion to follow the lead of their father, and join heartily in the work of breaking up their homes and leaving their native land forever. The parent had infused the children with his notions of success and they were proud to know he was head of such an enterprise; that his anticipations and promises were not visionary, but would be more than realized, and that he would in the future be held to be a public benefactor. The letters of his wife, though generally of a business character, show some attachment to him and regard for his affairs, which were in much confusion after his departure. No mention is made of the daughters, with whom in all probability the bad blood existed. Her advice to him in his business relations is good, and if followed more closely, would have saved him much vexation.

In making preparations for his departure it was decided that "only such articles as were actually necessary to supply the wants of the emigrants could be transported, leaving those of convenience and luxury out of the question. Implements of husbandry, tools for mechanics, material for building, medicines for the sick, and sustenance for the healthy, together with a scanty supply of furniture and household goods, must find a place in the ship. The ship Griffin, Robert Griffith, master, was chartered and brought to London for repairs and to receive the cargo and passengers. An entry made by John Smith in one of the books of record (Salem No. 4) in the office of the Secretary of State, Trenton, N. J., shows part of the persons that came at that time: they were John Fenwick, his three daughters, Elizabeth, Ann, and Priscilla; John Adams, husband of Elizabeth of Reading, in Berks, weaver, and three children; Elizabeth, aged eleven years, Fenwick, nine years, and Mary, four years; Edward Champneys, husband of Priscilla of Thornbury, Gloucestershire, joiner, and two children, John and Mary. John Fenwick brought ten servants, Robert Twiner, Gervis Bywater, William Wilkinson, Joseph Worth, Michael Eaton, Elinor Geere, Sarah Hutchins, Ruth Geere, Zachariah Geere, and Ann Parsons.

Besides these he was accompanied by Mary White, the faithful nurse of his children, who had lived in his family several years before coming to America. Her attachment for the three daughters showed itself in her resolve to share their good or bad fortune in a strange land. Their father's house was her home, where she had entire charge, and so continued until his decease. These traits of character were fully appreciated by the Patroon, as he gave her a title in fee for five hundred acres of land, and five days before the date of his will executed a lease to her, as "Mary White, late of the parish of Bromble, in the County of Wilkes, spinster, now of Fenwick Grove," for Fenwick Grove, containing three thousand acres; to continue during her life and the life of her husband, "if any she have when she decease." In his will he makes frequent mention of her name, continuing his liberality and always expressing the utmost confidence in her honesty and uprightness [2] ...

The effect of the coming of this ship up the Delaware is thus described in Clement's Life of John Fenwick. The account shows that the local political affairs were somewhat mixed.

While thus contemplating the development of his enterprise, a cloud, darker and more portentous than any before, showed itself; and from a direction not altogether unexpected by the chief proprietor or those who had accompanied him across the sea. The coming of a ship into the Delaware River, in 1675, was not an event to pass unnoticed by the Commander at New Castle, who, with the Justices, represented Governor Andros and his council, appointed by the Duke of York under his second patent from the King. The instructions to the Commander were to keep strict watch over the interests of His Royal Highness on both sides of the river, and, if anything should occur, to report at once to the authorities at New York. The ship in question proved to be the Griffin, anchored at Fort Elseborg, with English emigrants from London under the leadership of John Fenwick, who held the title to part of the territory on the Eastern shore, with the right of government derived through John Lord Berkeley and the Duke of York from the King. Further inquiry developed the fact that these people proposed to occupy the land on the Eastern side of the river, and establish a government for themselves under the right before named. This being properly brought to their knowledge, a court was convened in the fort at New Castle, and after due deliberation it was decided to forward, by express, the necessary information to the authorities at New York, and await orders therefrom. The express was no doubt a swift-footed Indian, selected for the purpose, who forded the river at the falls (Trenton) and continued by land through the forest to Communipaw; thence by water to the fort at New Amsterdam, where the message was delivered to his excellency, Governor Andros. The information was received December 5, 1675, and somewhat stirred the bile of the new executive, who held his commission direct and fresh from the Duke of York; and following the spirit and letter of his instructions, could not recognize any equal, or superior authority, within the limits of his jurisdiction. The Governor consulted his council, and an order was returned that John Fenwick and his followers be not recognized as having any rights, but be allowed to remain and occupy suitable portions of land under this government. The same express carried the reply, which the Commander at New Castle soon forwarded to John Fenwick and the adventurers and emigrants who were with him; intimating very strongly that they were regarded as intruders and enemies. That the title to the soil of New Jersey and the right of government as well, which was claimed to have passed by the grant from the Duke to Carteret and Berkeley, and under which John Fenwick held, was, by the Dutch conquest rendered inoperative and void; that the second patent of the King to the Duke restored the original elements of title and government as by him held in the first patent, and that like grants must come from His Royal Highness, as in the former case, to make any rights good on the Eastern shore of the Delaware River; that the government, as by Governor Andros and his council administered, was the only legitimate one within the boundaries given in his commission, and that he should expect all persons living therein to submit to the laws or suffer the penalty of transgressing them. To all this the Chief proprietor, as the owner of the territory, made a dignified response, showing whence he derived his title both to soil and government, which he regarded as sufficient and by which he determined to stand or fall. He insisted that his right to establish methods of government and the enactment and enforcement of laws, emanated from the same fountain as that of Governor Andros, had the advantage of priority in date, and needed no confirmation or endorsement by Governor Andros as the representative of the Duke of York. That these prerogatives had been before exercised and not questioned by the Crown, and, therefore, had nothing to concede or relinquish touching the demands made by the government at New Amsterdam. [3]

After two years of wrangling, in which the judgment of the courts were at first against Fenwick, the controversy finally subsided, leaving him in control of the land he had purchased and the colony he had founded. His recognized independence dates from the latter part of the year 1677.

Thus far he had continued to reside at Fenwick Grove until Salem County was organized, and indeed, until his death, which occurred in December, 1683. Mr. Clements has the following remarks and reflections upon the concluding period of his life: "On the second day of the third month, 1683, John Fenwick was returned as a member of the Colonial Assembly from the Salem tenth; but on account of ill health, which continued until his decease, he never sat as a member of that body. In this act is shown the complete absorption of the political rights and franchises, incident to the estate held in the ten lots, by the colonial authorities of West New Jersey and which appears to have been brought about peacefully and for the evident good of all concerned. This end was foreshadowed in the previous signing of the concessions and agreements by very many of the land owners, who held titles from Fenwick, and who had heretofore given their adherence to his government as established in 1675, but joined their fortunes with the more numerous colony and made common cause in advancing religious and political equality; to be enjoyed by all who ventured across the sea and fixed their homes within the limits of West New Jersey."

Here terminated the first form of a representative government established by the people. Rude and ill-defined as it was, sufficient appears to show that only time and occasion were wanting to develop its several parts, and secure to all the blessings to be derived from like institutions. The government established by the owners of the ninety parts was like in substance, but yielded to the people no greater privileges, nor more enlarged rights. This cannot but be interesting to those who care to trace the beginning of our present political institutions, and study the gradual but positive development of a system that has its foundation in the hearts of the people; to discover that no retrograde step had been taken in the fundamental doctrines of private or public rights and that a jealous care had been exercised that none be infringed.

The Patroon, in his manner of living, was more pretentious and aristocratic than any of his neighbors. His houses at Ivy Point and at Fenwick Grove were well appointed; proving that he had an eye to the creature comforts as well as to dignity and exclusiveness. The day had not come for wheeled carriages in the Salem tenth, but his stable included good saddle horses, with everything complete for the equestrian. A favorite road animal, "Jack," he makes special mention of in his will, and puts him in care of his trusty servant, Mary White, "who I desire to take care of him and see that he be not wronged as long as he liveth." His education as a cavalry officer in the army of the Commonwealth now served him, and however much he may have wished to discard the memories of his fighting days, yet in the saddle his grace and confidence as a rider could but be noticed. The library of books at each place he regarded with much interest, and directed their preservation after his decease; and touching his private papers he charges his executors with their care, and especially that they be not taken out of the colony. His agreement with the resident purchasers he wished to have religiously carried out and was anxious that his executors should see to the discharge of every obligation. His plantation at Fenwick Grove had many attractions for him, it being several miles from Ivy Point, where he could enjoy his leisure and look after his farming interests. He was systematic in his business affairs and always knew from his accounts whether a matter in hand was profitable or otherwise. For the day in which he lived, his agricultural operations were extensive and yielded a fair return. He does not appear to have had any slaves, but employed several persons about the estate, the whole being under his general superintendence. In the autumn of 1683, his health failing, he accepted an invitation from his favorite daughter, Ann, and placed himself under her care at Hedgefield, where he died in December of the same year. Her devotion to him remained the same through all the vicissitudes of his life, and with filial affection she cared for him on his dying bed.

Although in the depths of an American forest, and far from the land of his nativity, yet there were those around him in whose veins flowed his own blood, whose sympathies were enlisted for his welfare, but who were soon called upon to mourn his death. In him passed away one of the most remarkable men of his day and generation. His early manhood was spent in the excitements and participations of a war that overthrew the government, and well nigh destroyed the nation; while his middle life and latter days were occupied in an enlarged philanthropy to benefit his fellow man, by giving scope to his energies, with the certainty of reward to himself, and through him to his descendants; with the title of his land freed from the tenures of the feudal system, and without restraints, save those based in equity and good government.

In relation to the final disposition of his remains, he requested in his will that they be interred at Fenwick Grove. For some reason this was not complied with, as he was buried in "Sharp's family burying ground," long since abandoned for that use, and now nearly lost sight of. It is located near the present almshouse property of Salem County, overgrown with briers, and known to but few as the last resting place of the founder of Fenwick Colony.

Nearly two centuries have passed away, and not the rudest monument has been placed to show where his bones are laid. Generation after generation of his kin have neglected even to preserve a mound of earth to show his grave, and at this day "no man knoweth the place of his sepulchre." But a more enduring monument has survived him. His landed estate is covered with an industrious and happy people, in the enjoyment of free institutions, with no religious or political restraints; advanced in agriculture, commerce and manufactures, and participant in a degree of civilization that has no parallel in the world.

In his will, which is a curious and characteristic document, and bears date the seventh day of August, 1683, John Fenwick makes no mention of his wife, who was living in London at the time it was executed, and who appears to have had a separate estate which she used for her own comfort and convenience. This separation produced an indifference toward each other, which ended in a complete estrangement of feeling, and mutual disregard. Neither is there anything to show that she made claim on his estate or received from his executors or devisees any money arising therefrom. Nothing more is known of this relation, the lapse of time having obliterated every tradition in regard to it.

[1] Scribner's History United States, vol. ii, page 320, et seq.
[2] "To say that he [John Fenwick] was not a half brother to Charles II, king of England, would perhaps be assuming too much, although nothing appears to prove the affirmative of this assertion. The gallantries of the king were proverbial; hence the plausibility of the story and which by many came to be accepted as true. If, however, the royal blood colored his veins and infused into his character and disposition the idea of exclusiveness and authority, so palpable in many of his acts during life, it came from the first and not the last of these monarchs. The chance of such a story being true is too apparent to be denied, but may be accounted for in this wise. The first son of Charles Second, not recognized by law, was James, Duke of Monmouth, beheaded 1685, whose mother was Lucy Walters. James married Anne Scott, heiress of Buccleugh, whose second son married Elizabeth Fenwick, thus connecting the family with the blood royal, but several removes. Nothing short of a careful examination of the family genealogy in England will settle this point, which for the neglect may always remain a mooted question."

The above is quoted verbatim from John Clement's Life of John Fenwick. Charles II was born in 1630, at which time John Fenwick was twelve years of age, he having been born in 1618; hence Charles II is eliminated from the ancestry of

Fenwick. The remark: "The gallantries of the king were proverbial, etc.," refer to Charles II, and hence have but little bearing upon this question. By "the first" and "last" of these monarchs, the writer evidently means Charles I and Charles II. To be a half-brother of Charles II, Fenwick would have to be a son of Charles I. Charles I was born in 1600 and hence was eighteen years of age when John Fenwick was born. So far as I have seen there is no trace of relationship existing between him and the mother of Fenwick. John was the second son of Sir William Fenwick, baronet, the brothers being Edward, John, Roger, and Ralph.

The testimony of historians generally is to the effect that Charles I was a man of "strict decorum of conduct"; a man in "his private character of cultivated mind, kind, and of irreproachable life," and that "Ills personal morality was of the highest." To assume that Fenwick might be the illegitimate son of Charles I because Charles II was dissolute is altogether gratuitous. Besides, if it were so, Fenwick would have become the executioner of his own father, which is preposterous.
[3] Clement's Life of Fenwick.

Chapter Three - Fenwick Colony; Land Grants and Primary Government

The extensive grant of territory made by Charles II, the English king, to his brother, the Duke of York, was by royal charter dated twentieth of March, 1664. Upon the twenty-third of June in the same year, the Duke conveyed a portion of this territory to two other persons — John Lord Berkeley and Sir George Carteret. The conveyance to these individuals was made by an instrument in form as follows:

This indenture, made the three-and-twentieth day of June, in the sixteenth year of the Raigne of our Sovreign Lord Charles the Second, by the Grace of God, of England, Scotland, France and Ireland, King, Defender of the Faith — Anno Domini, 1664, between his Royal Highness, James, Duke of York and Albany, Earl of Ulster, Lord High Admiral of England and Ireland, Constable of Dover Castle, Lord Warden of the Cinque Ports and Governor of Portsmouth of the one part, John Lord Berkeley, Baron of Stratton and one of his majesties' most honorable privy Council and Sir George Carteret of Sattrum in the County of Devon, Knight, and one of his majesties' privy Council, of the other part, Witnesseth that said James, Duke of York, for and in consideration of the sum of ten shillings of lawful money of England, to him in hand paid, by these presents doth bargain and sell unto the said John Lord Berkeley and Sir George Carteret, all that tract of land adjacent to New England, and lying and being to the Westward of Long Island, bounded on the East part by the main sea, and part by Hudson's river, and hath upon the West Delaware Bay or river, and extendeth Southward to the mam ocean as far as Cape May at the mouth of Delaware Bay, and to the Northward as far as the Northernmost branch of said bay or river of Delaware, which is in forty-one degrees and forty minutes of latitude, and worketh over thence in a straight line to Hudson's river, which said tract of land is hereafter to be called by the name or names of Nova Cesarea, or New Jersey. [4]

Lord Berkeley and Sir George Carteret, thus becoming the proprietors of New Jersey, formed a constitution for the colony, and this was the first constitution of New Jersey. This instrument was entitled, "The concessions and agreement of the Lords Proprietors of the province of New Cesarea or New Jersey, to and with all and every of the new adventurers, and as such as shall settle or plant there." [5]

Lord Berkeley, soon becoming dissatisfied with his adventure, offered his share for sale, and this, as before stated, was purchased by John Fenwick and Edward Byllinge, members of the Society of Friends. The conveyance was executed to John Fenwick, in trust for Edward Byllinge, for the sum of one thousand pounds, and the tract thus purchased was afterward known as West New Jersey.

Besides the emigrants before mentioned, who arrived in the ship Griffith with John Fenwick, were also Edward Wade, Samuel Hedge, Samuel Wade, John Smith and wife, Samuel Nichols, Richard Guy, Richard Noble, a surveyor, Richard Hancock, also a surveyor, John Pledger, Hipolite Lufever, and John Matlock. These came over in this, the first English ship that came to West Jersey and none followed for nearly two years.

From this little group descended many, whose families are scattered over this part of the State, but who can now hardly trace their descent back to them.

John Matlock is said to have been the son of Abram Matlock, founder of Matlock College in England, and from him descended the Matlock families of this and Gloucester Counties. In Gloucester County some of the members still retain the name of Matlock, while in this county the name is spelled Matlack. E. L. Matlack, an auctioneer and farmer of Cumberland County, is said to be a lineal descendant.

Fenwick and Byllinge, becoming sole proprietors, were styled "Lord Proprietors," and when Fen wick's tenth was set off to him and his connection with Byllinge became dissolved he became "Lord Proprietor" of West New Jersey, and was so styled, and the Goulds' tradition a hundred years ago was "We descended from Lord Fenwick." [The writer of this, now over threescore and ten years of age, has heard the words from his grandparents, and other of the Goulds who were born and lived in the close of the eighteenth century.] That there is pretty conclusive ground for giving credence to this tradition, will be shown later.

The proprietors, increasing in numbers by purchase of land from trustees under arrangements with William Penn, Gauen Laurie, and Nicholas Lucas, agreed upon a form of government comprising many of the provisions of the instrument formed by Berkeley and Carteret, together with others originating with themselves. This was styled "The concessions and agreements of the proprietors, freeholders and inhabitants of the province of West New Jersey." An extract from this instrument (Chapter III) reads:

That hereafter upon the furthest settlement of the said province, the proprietors and inhabitants, resident upon the said province, shall and may, at or upon the first and twentieth day of the month called March, which shall be in the year, according to the English account, one thousand six hundred and eighty; and so thence forward upon the said day, assemble themselves together, in some public place to be ordered and appointed by the Commissioners for the time being, and upon default of such appointment, in such place as they shall see meet, and then and there elect of and amongst themselves, ten honest and able men, fit for government, to officiate and execute the place of commissioners for the year ensuing, and until such time as ten more, for the year then next following shall be elected and appointed; which said elections shall be as follows; that is to say, the inhabitants each ten of the one hundred proprietors, shall elect and choose one, and the one hundred proprietors shall be divided into ten divisions or tribes of men. And the said elections shall be made and distinguished by balloting trunks, to avoid noise and confusion, and not by voices, holding up of the hands, or otherwise howsoever, which said commissioners, so yearly to be elected, shall likewise govern and order the affairs of the said province (pro tempore) for the good and welfare of the said people, and according to these our concessions, until such time as the general free assembly shall be elected and deputed in such manner and wise as is hereafter expressed and contained. [6]

The Swedes and Finns had settled in what became Salem and Gloucester Counties long before the arrival of Fenwick, superseding the Dutch, who had largely disappeared from the section. There was, no doubt, a considerable sprinkling of this population occupying the territory before Fenwick arrived. Johnson, in his History, says "The Swedes and Finns arrived in 1627, the Dutch having left the country. In 1631 they built a fort at Finn's Point." Judge Elmer states in his History of Cumberland County, "A few of the New Haven people, who as early as 1641 made a settlement on the creek called by the Dutch Varchen's Kill (now Salem Creek), may have wandered into the limits of Cumberland, thus becoming the pioneers of the considerable number, who about fifty years later came from Connecticut, Rhode Island, and Long Island."

Fenwick arrived in 1675 in the English ship, "Griffith" bringing with him the persons some of whom have been already named, as follows: "Arriving after a good passage, he landed at a pleasant, rich spot, situated near Delaware, by him called Salem, probably from the peaceable aspect it then bore. He brought with him three daughters and many servants; two of whom, Samuel Hedge and John Adams, afterward married his daughters. The other passengers were Edward Champness, who married Priscilla, Fenwick's third daughter (this name Champness will appear in connection with the Goulds), Edward Wade, Samuel Wade, John Smith and wife, Samuel Nichols, Richard Guy, Richard Noble, Richard Hancock, John Pledger, Hipolite Lefever, and John Matlock. This was the first English ship which came to West Jersey, and none followed for near two years, owing probably to a difference between Fenwick and Byllinge." — Historical Collection of New Jersey.

Before the arrival of the second ship from London, the "Kent," Gregory Marlow, master, the constitution or form of government before referred to was made, which was entitled: "The concessions and agreements of the proprietors, freeholders, and inhabitants of the province of West New Jersey." This constitution is witnessed and signed in the following manner, according to "Historical Collections":

In testimony and witness of our consent to and affirmation of these present laws, concessions, and agreements, we, the proprietors, freeholders, and inhabitants of the said province of West New Jersey, whose names are underwritten, have to the same voluntarily and freely set our hands, dated this third day of the month, commonly called March, in the year of our Lord, one thousand six hundred seventy-six. — Gawen Lawrie, Wm. Penn, Wm. Euily, Josh. Wright, Wm. Haig, Wm. Peachee, Rich. Matthews, John Harris, Francis Collins, Wm. Kent, Benj. Scot, John Penford, Tho. Lambert, Tho. Hooten, Henry Stacy, Edw. Byllinge, Rich. Smith, Edward Thelthorp, Dan. Wills, Thomas Olive, Tho. Rudgard, William Riddle, Robert Stacy, John Farrington, Wm. Royden, Rich. Mew, Percival Towle, Mahlon Stacy, Tho. Budd, Sam, Jennings, John Lambert, Will. Heulings, George Deacon, John Thomson, Edward Bradway, Richard Guy, James Nevell, William Cantwell, Fospe Outstout, Machgijel Baron, Casper Herinow, Turrse Psese, Robert Kemble, John Corneliesse, Gerrat Van Jumne, William Gill Johnson, Mich. Lackerouse, Markus Algus, Evert Aldricks, Hendrick Everson, Jilles Fonieson, Caas Jansen, Paul Doequet, Aert Jansen, John Surige, Tho. Smith, James Pearce, Edw, Webb, John Pledger, Richard Wilkinson, Christe Sanders, Renear Van Horst, William Johnson, Charles Bogler, Samuel Wade, Thomas Woodruff, John Smith, Tho. Pierce, William Warner, Joseph Ware, Isaac Smart, Andrew Thompson, Thomas Kent, Henry Jennings, Richard Wortsaw, Christopher White, John Maddocks, John Forrest, James Nickory, William Rumsey, Richard Robinson, Mark Reeve, Thomas Watson, Samuel Nicholson, Daniel Smith, Richard Daniels, William Fenton, William Darine, Robert Zane, Walter Peiterson, Anthony Page, Andrew Borthesen, Wooley Woollison, Anthony Dixon, John Derme, Thomas Benson, John Pain, Richard Brillington, Samuel Lovett, Henry Stubbins, William Willis, George Hazelwood, Roger Pedrick, William Hughes, Van Highst, Hipotas Lefever, William Wilkinson, Andrew Shenneck, Lanse Cornelicus, Samuel Hedge, William Mossier, John Grubb, John Worlidge, Edward Meyer, Thomas Borton, Robert Powel, Thomas Hording, Matthew Allen, Bernard Devenish, Thomas Stokes, Thomas French, Isaac Marriott, John Butcher, George Hutchinson, Thomas Gardner, Thomas Eves, John Borton, John Paine, Eleazer Fenton, Samuel Oldale, William Black, Anthony Woodhouse, Daniel Leeds, John Pancoast, Francis Belwicke, William Luswall, John Snowdon, Richard Fenemore, Gruna Jacobson, Thomas

Scholey, Thomas Might, Godfrey Hancock, John Petty, Abraham Heulings, John Newboald, John White, John Roberts, John Wood, John Hosling, Thomas Revell.

These numerous signatures clearly show that there was a considerable population already in the country, but with regard to the lands of Salem County, if not of the major part of this section of west New Jersey, Fenwick was doubtless the sole proprietor. He made deeds and sold lands in the province, both before and after his arrival in the country. An original parchment deed, now in the possession of Orestes Cook, Esq., of Bridgeton, New Jersey, shows that he either executed this deed in England, or else he arrived in America before June, 1675. This deed, a copy of which follows, was written and executed May tenth, sixteen hundred and seventy-five, and it was signed and sealed with Fenwick's own hand and before the witnesses named. This deed was for five hundred acres of land contained in "all that Moyetie or half part of the tract of land called New Cesarea or New Jersey," which Fenwick bought of Lord John Berkeley by "Indenture bearing date the eighteenth day of March, sixteen hundred and seventy-three," and conveys the said five hundred acres to Richard Hancock (who became Fen wick's surveyor general at first). This deed does not locate the land sold to Hancock.

It is a curious manuscript, beautifully written and well preserved.

Out of this tract Richard Hancock sold one hundred acres to John Denn, by deed dated February twelfth, sixteen hundred and eighty-two; this land is located by butts and bounds, as will be seen, and is along Alloway's Creek. This original parchment is also in the possession of Mr. Cook.

Both deeds are given in full in Chapter IV. They will probably find their way soon into the Cumberland County Historical Society.

There is also still in existence a deed of Fenwick's son-in-law, John Adams, to Samuel Bacon for two hundred and sixty acres of land, in Bacon's Neck, made by Adams in sixteen hundred and eighty-two. This John Adams was the father of Elizabeth Adams, the mother of the original Gould, the founder of Gouldtown. He later purchased one thousand acres in Alloway's. The deed, Fenwick to Hancock, and Hancock to Denn, follows in the next chapter.

[4] This appears to be the first instrument in which the bounds of New Jersey are regularly defined. — Historical Collections of New Jersey.
[5] Printed in Salem Records, in N. J. archives from the original parchment brought over from Europe by John Fenwick in 1675.
[6] Historical Collections of New Jersey.

Chapter Four - Copies of Very Ancient Parchment Deeds in Possession of a Bridgeton Attorney Deed

John Fenwick to Richard Hancock. May 10, 1675.

To all people to whom this present writing shall come:
John Fenwick, late of Binfields, in the County of Berkshire, within the Kingdom of England, Esquire, and Chiefe Proprietor of the Moyetie or half part of the tract of land within the Province of New Cesaria or New Jersey — in America — sendeth greeting.

Whereas, the Honorable John Lord Berkeley of Stratton, one of his Majesties most honorable Privy Counsell, by his Indenture bearing date the eighteenth day of March, one thousand six hundred seventy and three — did grant, bargain, sell, alien and enfeoff and confirm unto the said John Fenwick, his heirs and assigns forever, all that Moyetie or halfe part of the tract of land called New Cesaria or New Jersey, and also the rivers, rivolets, mines, mineralls, quaries, woods, royalties, profits, franchises, conditions, comodities and other hereditaments whatsoever, in the said Indenture, particularly mentioned, as in and by the same relaçon being thereunto had may appear.

Now know yee, that for and in consideration of the summ of Sixty Shillings, lawful money of England to him, the said John Fenwick in hand paid by Richard Hancock, of Bromley, Neer Bow, in the County of Midd'x, upholsterer at and before the ensealing and delivery hereof, the receipt whereof is hereby assured, bargained and for other diver considerations, him, the said John Fenwick hereunto moving, he, the said John Fenwick, hath granted, bargained, sold, aliened, enfeoffed and confirmed - unto the said Richard Hancock and his wife, and the heirs and assigns of the said Richard Hancock forever, Five Hundred acres of land, to be taken out of, sett forth and surveyed out of all such part of the said tract of land within the Province of New Cesaria or New Jersey, the said John Fenwick hath reserved to him and his heirs forever, hereafter to be called Fenwick Colony, and alsoe all river, rivolets, mines, mineralls, quarries, woods, proffits, commodities and hereditaments, whatsoever, to the said Five Hundred Acres belonging and all the estate right, title, interest, property, claim and demand whatsoever of him, the said John Fenwick, of, in, or to the said five hundred acres, and premises herein before men9oned or intended to be bargained and sold or any part or parcell thereof and the rendition, renditions, remainder and remainders thereof to have and to hold the said Five Hundred acres of land and all and singular the premises herein before mençoned intended to be granted, bargained, sold, aliened, enfeoffed and confirmed, with the appurtenances and every part and parcel thereof, unto the said Richard Hancock and Margaret, his wife, and the heirs and assigns of the said Richard Hancock forever to the only use and behoof of the said Richard Hancock and Margaret, his wife, and the heirs and assigns of the said Richard Hancock forever, yeeilding and paying therefor the yearly rent of ears of Indian com on the nine and twentieth day of the seventh month, called September, and the said John Fenwick, for himselfe, his heirs, executors, administrators and assigns, doth covenant and grant to and with Richard Hancock and Margaret, his wife, and the heirs and assigns of the said Richard Hancock by these presents — that they, the said Richard Hancock and Margaret, his wife, and the heirs and assigns of the said Richard Hancock, shall and may hold and enjoy the said Five Hundred acres and premises and receive and have the rents, issues and proffits thereof from time to time without the let, erection or disturbance of him the said John Fenwick — John Lord Berkeley — Sir George Cartaret — Knight and Baronet — Chief Proprietor of the other Moyetie of the said tract of land or any or either of them, their or any or either of their heirs or assigns, or of, or by any other person or persons claiming or to claim by, from or under him, them or either of them and for and in respect of any right or interests which he or they or any or either of them shall or may have or claim unto said Five Hundred acres of land soe granted as aforesaid, or any part or parcell thereof, and not otherwise freed and discharged or otherwise suffitionly saved harmless of and from all incumbrances whatsoever done or suffered by him, them or any or either of them in the meantime.

In witness whereof, the said John Fenwick hath hereunto set his hand and seale this tenth day of the third month called May, in the year of our Lord Christ, One thousand six hundred seventy and five and in the twenty-seaventh year of the Reyne of King Charles the second, over England, Scotland, France and Ireland, &c.

(*Facsimile*)
BACK.
Signed, sealed and delivered in the presence of us
John Elridge, Edward Wade, Edmund Warner,
Thomas Anderson, Edward Bradway, Richard Noble.

Enrolled in the Register Book of Deeds and conveyances belonging and Fenwick Colony in the Province of New Cesaria or New Jersey in America, in the third month called May, MDCLXXV. GARFIELD.

DEED.

Richard Hancock and Margaret, his wife, *to* John Denn and Margaret, his wife.
February 12, 1682.

To all people to whom this present writing shall come:
Richard Hancock of Alloway's Creek, in the Province of West New Jersey, Yeoman, sendeth greeting.

Whereas, John Fenwick, late one of the Proprietors of the said Province by his Deed Poll, bearing date the tenth day of May, sixteen hundred and seventy-five, did grant, bargain, sell, alien, enfeoffe and confirme unto said Richard Hancock, late of Bromley, County of Midd'x, upholsterer, to five hundred acres of land to be taken, set forth, and surveyed out of that tract of land, which he, the said John Fenwick had referred to him and his heirs forever. Within the said province and also the rivers, rivoletts, woods, quaries, mines, minerals, profitts, commoodies, hereditaments, whatsoever unto the said Five Hundred acres of land belonging in the said deed particularly mentioned as in and by the same relation being had may appeare.

Now know yee, that for and in consideration of sum of Five pounds, warrant pay of Delaware River to him, the said Richard Hancock, in hand paid by John Denn, of Allowayes Creeke, at and before the ensealing and delivery thereof, the receipt whereof is hereby acknowledged and for divers other causes and considerations him, the said Richard Hancock thereunto moving, the said Richard Hancock, hath granted, bargained and sold, aliened and enfeoffed, and confirmed unto the said John Denn and Margaret, his wife, and to the heirs and assignes of the said John Denn forever, one hundred acres of land, part and parcel of the said five hundred acres, butted and bounded as followeth, (viz) Beginning at a great Tree standing neere Munmouth River, alis Alloway's Creeke aforesaid, mark't with R. U. K. and J. S. from thence by North and by East upon a Strait lyne and by the markt trees that leads to a tree with J. D. three hundred and twenty pearches; from thence upon a straite line West and by North to a tree markd J. D. fifty pearches; from thence South by West by the marked treese that leeads to the middle of the highway or lane the parte of the plantations and so downe the midle of the highway to the said creek or riverside, three hundred and twenty pearches, from thence Easterly up the said Creeke or river to the first mentioned tree fifty pearches, within the bounds are contained one hundred acres of fast land, marish and swamp, be it more or lesse as by a certificate and in the hand of the said Richard Hancock, bearing date eighth day of February, last appear. And all the house, improvement, woods, rivers, creeks, quaries, mines, mineralls, profitts, commodities, and hereditaments whatsoever, to the said one hundred acres belonging and all the estate, right, title, interest, property, claime and demand whatsoever of the said Richard Hancock and Margret, his wife, of, in, or to the said one himdred acres of land and premises herein before mentioned or intended to be granted, bargained, sold, aliened, enfeofed and confirmed, any part or parcel thereof.

And the reverçon, reverçons, remainder and remainders thereof to have and to hold the said one hundred acres of land, house, improvement, woods, rivers, creeks, quaries, mines, minerals, profitts, comodities, and hereditaments, thereunto belonging herein and hereby granted, bargained, sold, aliened, enfeoffed and confirmed every part and parcel thereof unto him the said John Denn and Magret his wife, and to the heirs and assignes, of him, the said John Denn forever, to the only use and behoofe of him, the said John Denn and Margret, his wife, their heires and assigns forever, yeilding and paying therefor yearly and every yeare unto the said Richard Hancock, his heires and assignes, the yearely rent of one eare of indian come on the nine and twentieth day of September, if demanded, and the said Richard Hancock, for himselfe, and Margret, his wife, and for his heires and assignes, doth covenant and grant to and with the said John Denn and Margret, his wife, by these presents, that he, the said John Denn and Margret, his wife, and the heires and assignes of the said John Denn, shall and may hold and enjoy the said one hundred acres of land and premises, and receive and take the rents, issues and profits thereof from time to time without the let, erection or disturbance of him, the said Richard Hancock and Margret, his wife, and the said John Fenwick or any or either of them, their or any or either of their heires or assignes or of any other person or persons, claiming or to claime by or under him, them or any or either of them for or in respect of any right, title or interest, which they or any or either of them shall or may have or claime upon, or to the said one hundred acres of land, house, improvements and premises so granted aforesaid, or any part or parcel thereof freed and discharged or otherwise well and sufficiently saved harmless of and from all incumbrances whatsoever, done or suffered by him, them or any or either of them in meantime.

In witness whereof, the said Richard Hancock for himself and for Magaret, his late wife, deceased, hath hereunto set his hand and seals, this twelfth day of February, sixteen hundred and eighty-two.

Signed Richard Hancock.

Signed, sealed and delivered in the presence of James Nevill, Edward Wade, Comr's.

endorsed
John Denn's deed for 100 acres from Rich'd Hancock.

This deed indicates the location of Hancock's five hundred acres conveyed by the first deed.

Chapter Five - Gould Traditions; Evidences; Descent; Benjamin Gould's Will

Extract from Fenwick's will: "Item, I do except against Elizabeth Adams of having any ye leaste part of my estate, unless the Lord open her eyes to see her abominable transgression against him, me and her good father, by giving her true repentance, and forsaking yt Black yt hath been ye ruin of her, and becoming penitent for her sins; upon yt condition only I do will and require my executors to settle five hundred acres of land upon her." (Lucius Q. C. Elmer, History of Cumberland County, N. J., 1869.)

Judge Elmer was born in 1793 and died in 1883; he was the son of General Ebenezer Elmer, who was born in 1752 and died in 1843; he was the youth who accompanied his father. General Elmer, on Sunday afternoons to the little school house in Gouldtown which was also used as a church, in which the Goulds, Pierces, and Murrays, mulattoes, and Woodruffs, Westcotts, Seeleys, Batemans, and Fullers, white, held religious worship. The house is still standing, though moved to another locality. The children were catechized here; and Judge Elmer has often related how he once asked Othniel Murray, one of the small boys, what was the first thing he did when he arose in the morning, and the boy replied, "I go to my traps." The expected answer was an allusion to his morning devotions.

In Evarts and Peck's "History of Salem, Cumberland, and Gloucester Counties," published a few years ago, a sketch of Gouldtown appears which says:

Gouldtown is a settlement of colored people, many of them nearly white, about three miles east of Bridgeton. The families there mostly bear the names of Pierce and Gould. Some of them are active, industrious farmers, and have accumulated considerable property. A tradition believed by many is, that they are descended from Elizabeth Adams, the granddaughter of Fenwick — who directed in his will that his executors settle five hundred acres of land upon her on conditions stated. Fenwick made his will and died in 1683. The tradition among the inhabitants of Gouldtown is that Elizabeth married Gould from whom they descended and that the five hundred acres of land was settled upon her and they inherited it.

From these statements it will be seen that a persistent and well spread "tradition" prevailed that the Goulds were descendants of Fenwick.

John Adams who had married Elizabeth Fenwick had a daughter Elizabeth, who was eleven years old at the time of the arrival of the family in Jersey and who consequently was nineteen years old at the time Fenwick made his will excepting against her having any share of his property unless she should repent of her sins and forsake "that Black that hath been the ruin of her."

Judge Lucius Q. C. Elmer

Johnson's History of Fenwick's Colony, written in 1835, and published in 1839, says: "Among the numerous troubles and vexations which assailed Fenwick, none appear to have distressed him more than the base and abandoned conduct of his granddaughter, Elizabeth Adams, who had attached herself to a citizen of color. By his will he deprives her of any share in his estate, 'unless the Lord open her eyes to see her abominable transgression against him, me and her good father, by giving her true repentance and forsaking that Black which hath been the ruin of her and becoming penitent for her sins.' From this illicit connection has sprung the families of the Goulds at a settlement called Gouldtown, in Cumberland County." Later, this same historian in a memoir of John Fenwick wrote: "Elizabeth Adams had formed a connection with a negro man whose name was Gould." [7]

This John and Elizabeth Adams continued to live in what is now Cumberland County after the death of Fenwick; but the historians give no further mention of Elizabeth Gould, if indeed she ever took the name of Gould. John and Elizabeth Adams possessed land in what is now Bacon's Neck in Cumberland County acquired through John Fenwick and in the year before the death of the latter, sold two hundred and sixty acres to Samuel Bacon, a Quaker and seaman from Woodbridge, New Jersey; hence the name Bacon's Neck. The deed for this property is still in existence among the papers of the late Mrs. Kate Knight and now in the possession of Ephraim J. Cook, of Port Norris, N. J.

John Adams appears to have been unable to write, as all the public documents signed by him are by "his mark." Then Elizabeth Adams, senior, according to this will, was living in 1682, although John Clements supposes she had died before her father's will was made in 1683. This supposition is based upon the fact that she is not mentioned in the will and that the devises therein made are directly to her children. John Adams died in 1700.

The name of the Gould whom Elizabeth married is not known, nor is the date of her death, or the place where she is buried. We have the record of only one son, and of him we have but two authentic records.

In the oldest register of the Gouldtown graveyard the spot is marked where is laid away the remains of, "Benjamin Gould and Ann, his wife." Swedes and Finns had been settled in some parts of what is now Salem and Gloucester Counties before Fenwick's arrival, and this Benjamin Gould's wife, Ann, was a Finn.

The following is his will. The name is spelled Gold, Goold and Gould, in the records.

WILL OF BENJAMIN GOULD.

SECRETARY OF STATE'S OFFICE, TRENTON, NEW JERSEY, BOOK 18 OF WILLS, PAGE 516.

In the Name of God, Amen, the ninth day of May, in the year of our Lord, 1777.

I, Benjamin Gold, of Fairfield, in the County of Cumberland and in the State of New Jersey, yeoman, being sick and weak in body, but of perfect mind and memory, blessed be God therefor, calling unto mind the Mortallity of my body and knowing that it is appointed unto all men once to die do make and ordain this my last will, that is to say, principally and first of all give and recommend my soul into the hands of God, who gave it and for my body I recommend it to the Earth to be buried in a Christianlike and decent manner at the discretion of my executors, nothing doubting but at the general Resurrection I shall receive the same again by the mighty power of God and as touching such worldly estate wherewith it hath pleased God to bless me in this life I give, devise and dispose of in the following manner and form:

Imprimis: It is my will and I do order that in the first place all my just debts and funeral charges be paid and satisfied in some convenient time after my decease by my executors.

Item: I give, and bequeath unto my well beloved wife, Ann Gold, the one-third part of all my moveable estate to her and her heirs forever and also the third part of the profits of my plantation on which I now dwell at the West end of my land.

Item: I give and bequeath unto my daughter, Sarah Goold, one small feather bed to her and her heirs forever.

Item: I give and bequeath unto my eldest son, Anthony Goold, the sum of Fifteen pounds to be paid to him out of my moveable estate to him and to his heirs forever, and I do order that a Vendue shall be made of all my moveable estate and when my debts are paid out of it and my wife has got her thirds out of it as aforesaid, the remainder of my moveable estate to be equally divided between my two sons, Samuel Goold and Abijah Goold.

Item: I give and bequeath unto my two sons, Samuel Goold and Abijah Goold One hundred and thirty-six acres of my land on the East end to be equally divided between them. I give it to them and to their heirs forever.

Item: I give and bequeath unto my youngest son, Elisha Goold, all the remainder of my land to him and his heirs forever. And I do constitute make and ordain Thomas Joslin with James Hood my only and sole executors of this my last will and testament and do hereby utterly disallow revise and disallow all and every other former testaments, wills, legacies and executors ratifying this and no other to be my last will and testament.

In witness whereof, I have hereunto set my hand and seal the day and year above written.

Benjamin Goold. (*Seal*)

Witnesses
    James Sayre, Joshua White,
        her
    Anna X Sayre.
        mark.

The date of probate is not given, but the preceding was proven June 27, 1777. The account of the executors was approved February 13, 1779 (Book 22, page 69). It amounted to £148 5s., personal.

Anthony Gould left a will (Book 40, page 508), dated June 23, 1803. Witnesses, Jeremiah Smith, Abner Smith. It directs all property to be sold — to daughter Phebe Gould $6. Remainder to be divided between two daughters, Christiana and Martha. Jonathan Bowen, Executor, and guardian of daughters, Christiana and Martha until they are eighteen. Will proved September 27, 1803. Anthony Gould was Benjamin's oldest son.

From these four sons, mentioned in the above will, descended all the Goulds of Gouldtown, and from them the place derived its name.

When Benjamin Gould, the founder of Gouldtown, grew up, it is quite probable there were no girls of his own color with whom he could associate had he desired to do so; that he had brothers and sisters to grow to maturity has not been established, but the tradition handed down through his sons is that his parents had five children, one of whom was a son named Levi; all the others died young, and all trace of Levi was lost before the death of Benjamin. It was held that Levi was older than Benjamin.

Benjamin married a Finn, whose name was Ann; he got none of the Fenwick land, nor any of the lands of his mother's father, John Adams, so far as can be learned.

There were other descendants of both Fenwick and Adams, for Samuel Hedge and Edward Champness, as well as John Adams, married daughters of Fenwick.

Judge Elmer, in his history of Cumberland County says: "Benjamin Champneys (thus he spells the name) a descendant of Fenwick, studied with Ebenezer Elmer in 1793, and, after a few voyages at sea, married a daughter of Colonel Potter, and settled as a physician in Bridgeton. He was much esteemed, but died young in 1814."

The "Widow Champneys," mother of the Dr. Champneys mentioned, kept the Pole Tavern, one of the ancient landmarks of South Jersey; Dr. Champneys was her son. Colonel Potter's sons, whose sister Dr. Champneys married, kept a general store in Bridgeton, at which the Goulds, as well as the general public, dealt. One of the sons of a member of the firm has often repeated this little incident as showing that the claimed descent of the Goulds from Fenwick was known then as the common and undisputed tradition. He said that Dr. Champneys was connected with the store, and among those who had become indebted to the store was Benjamin Gould, second, the grandson of the founder of Gouldtown. This Benjamin Gould was a dealer in cord-wood and hoop-poles, to a considerable extent.

The firm sued him for the amount of an indebtedness which he had contracted with them. This made him, Gould, very angry, and he hastened to the store in great wrath that he should be treated with such indignity. After he had given vent to his feelings and had cooled off so he could be talked to in a pacific manner. Dr. Champneys said: "Well, Benjamin, we knew it was a mean thing to do, and we hated to do it, but we need money very badly and we've got to sue people to get it in, and we didn't know who to begin on; so we thought we would begin on our own relations first, then other people wouldn't mind it so much."

The explanation was entirely satisfactory and the account was settled. This incident was told to the writer by the son of the member of the firm alluded to, who, at the time of relating, was the acknowledged historiographer of local events and traditions, and a reliable local genealogist. The Benjamin Gould, second, was the grandfather of the writer; he was born in 1779, or two years after the death of his grandfather, Benjamin, first, and was, at the time of this incident, about thirty years old. He was the son of Abijah Gould, who died in 1806, who was born about 1730 or 1735.

Benjamin Gould, the founder, was born between 1700 and 1705; his mother, Elizabeth Adams Gould, being then a little more than thirty-five years of age.

Comparatively nothing is known of his early life; it is believed that he was the youngest of the five children. He must have been a hardy man of thrift, and a man much nearer white than mulatto, as indicated by his descendants. His will shows that he had accumulated considerable property, which is still in the hands of his descendants, who have added to it. The inventory of his personal property, consisting of cattle, sheep, oxen and the like, aggregated £148 5s., which was quite a sum for those days.

His will left £15 to his oldest son, Anthony. Why this was so does not appear, unless it was because he considered him already provided for, or had previously helped him, for all records in the County Clerk's Office show that Anthony Gould owned property on the road from Bridgetown to Beaver Dam, or Maurice River Bridge, which he had purchased from John Page, by deed bearing date 1767.

Benjamin Gould had three other sons and one daughter; the other sons, as given in the will, and whose descendants are all easily traced, were Samuel, Abijah and Elisha; the daughter, Sarah, died unmarried, shortly after the death of her father. The early life of these four boys was not altogether monotonous, they had plenty of companions among the hardy woodmen of those times, for the country was forest-covered, the principal source of industry being the cutting and hauling of logs, rails for fencing, cord-wood and timber.

[7] R. G. Johnson, Memoir of John Fenwick, in New Jersey Hist. Soc. Publ., 1849.

Chapter Six - The Early Goulds and Their Associations; the Pierces and Murrays; the Three Foundation Families

In "Historical Collections of New Jersey," it is related that Fenwick made three purchases from the Indians of the lands included in the tract out of which Salem and Cumberland Counties were made; the first and second purchases included all the country between the Cohansey and Salem creeks, and the third purchase included all which lay between the Cohansey and Maurice River. These purchases were made in the years 1675 and 1676. "Emigrants were now arriving and Fenwick, having become sole proprietor of this large tract of country, which he called Fenwick's colony, sales were rapidly made of large, as well as small tracts of land, and so continued until his death."

The following is extracted "From the First General Order, as agreed upon by Fenwick and the first purchasers":

And as for the settling of the town of New Salem, it is likewise ordered that the town be divided by a street; that the Southeast side be for the purchasers, who are to take their lots of sixteen acres as they come to take them up and plant them, as they happen to join to the lots of the purchasers resident, who are to hold their present plantations, and all of them to be accounted as part of their purchases, and the other part, on the North and by East and by South is to be disposed of by the chief proprietor for the encouragement of trade; he also giving, for the good of the town in general, the field or marsh that lieth between the town and Goodchild's plantation; ...and lastly, we do leave all other things concerning the setting forth and surveying the said purchases unto the chief proprietor, to order as he sees fit.

Signed accordingly, the twenty-fifth day of the fourth month, sixteen hundred and seventy-six.

Fenwick.

Edward Wade, John Smith, Richard Noble, Samuel Nicholson, John Adams, Hypolite Lefevre, Edward Champness, Richard Whitacar, William Malston, Robert Wade.

John Fenwick held much the same relation to this section of New Jersey — especially to Salem and Salem County — as William Penn did to Philadelphia and that portion of Pennsylvania.

We have now to do mainly with the lines of the three families whose names are mentioned in the opening chapter of this book. The beginning of the Gould family has been outlined sufficiently now to introduce the beginning of the two other families already named — the Pierces and the Murrays.

The Pierces were next in point of early intelligence and importance to the Goulds. Benjamin Gould and his four sons showed considerable broadmindedness, and intelligence, as will appear in further detail; they accumulated property, and maintained a life of independence, self-reliance, and manhood for the times in which they lived and the naturally poor soil and country which they inhabited. The white people who inhabited the contiguous localities fared no better than they, and those of them who achieved any greater success in life than did the Goulds of those early days, changed their locality before changing their mode of living. Before the material advancement in life and standing of these families now detailed, the entire country between what is now Bridgeton and Millville, had been surveyed and cut up into smaller holdings.

Judge Elmer's history shows that Richard Hancock, who was Fenwick's first Surveyor-General, came to what is now called Bridgeton in 1686 and erected a sawmill on the stream then called and ever since known as Mill Creek, which runs along by the Dix wrapper factory and is the outlet of East Lake and the Indian Field Run. This land, covered, as it then was, with heavy cedar, pine, and oak timber, was included in an eleven-thousand-acre survey, located about this time for the West Jersey Society. This Society was formed by several large proprietors living partly in London and partly in the provinces. Probably Hancock obtained title to his holdings from them, says Judge Elmer. Continuing he says: "It does not appear that he ever lived here, his residence being at the place in Salem County named after him Hancock's Bridge, where there still remain some of his descendants." From Hancock's sawmill much lumber was sawed up and sent away — for Thomas, a historian, states, says Judge Elmer, "a goodly store of lumber went out of the Cohansey to Philadelphia."

Writing of the eleven-thousand-acre survey, before mentioned, and as appears in Elmer's History, the records show that "on the east side of the Cohansey a large tract of eleven thousand acres was surveyed by Worlidge and Budd for the West Jersey Society in 1686, and this was resurveyed and recorded in 1716. East of that tract a large survey was made for the heirs of William Penn, which extended to the Maurice River. It has been asserted that the holdings of Benjamin Gould and his compatriots came originally from the West Jersey Society out of this eleven-thousand-acre survey. Elmer's History declares: "It may be safely said that four-fifths of the land included in Cumberland County was covered by surveys before 1700."

The first proprietors of the land within the bounds of what is now Cumberland County were principally Friends; but few of the actual settlers, however, were Friends; these people being mostly confined to Greenwich, and later, a few on Maurice River, about Buckshutem and vicinity and finally about where Millville now is.

It requires some stretch of imagination to understand how those hardy people, those pioneers and early settlers, made a living, — yet those who are now advanced to near the fourscore mark of their years can form a pretty good conception of their modes of life, as they gathered it from the traditions and conversations, jokes, anecdotes, and pleasantries of their own grandsires and granddames. The grandsires would tell about their daily life in clearing their lands, burning the logs or hauling them to the sawmill with their oxen; about sowing the rye for the rye bread, or the flax to grow their own clothing; instruct how to pull the flax, heckle it, spin it into thread and weave it into coarse tow cloth; how some raised sheep, sheared the wool, spun it, and had it woven into the coarse "linsey-woolsey" cloth, from which the granddames could make the heavy warm clothing of "homespun" and "bobinette." They would tell also of the leather breeches of calfskin and the under jackets made of deerskin; and of splint chairs, home-made, bottomed with the deerskin, the splint brooms with which they swept the floors of their humble homes, many of them mere cabins; the "noggins" and the "piggins" with which to measure small commodities; some would tell how they reaped the grain with the sickle, walking their oxen over it, treading out the grain on the threshing floors to winnow out afterward in the winds.

All these things I have heard related, and so have you, who have lived your threescore and ten years in Cumberland County. Such as this was the hardy and independent life of the early inhabitants of Gouldtown. The great forests fell beneath the strokes of their axes; the logs were hauled to the sawmill and the cordwood to the landings on the Cohansey River, whence they were taken in vessels either as lumber or cord-wood to Philadelphia; or the wood was burned to charcoal and taken to Philadelphia and New York, in those early days. There was but little charcoal, however, shipped from the landings on the Cohansey; most of this commodity was hauled to the landings on the Maurice River and shipped to New York, as that was the better market. There were landings on the Cohansey known as "The Bridge," afterward called "Cohansey Bridge" — now Bridgeton. "Free Landing," a point between the Dailey farm and the Donaghay farm, and also at "Bumbridge" — now Fairton. Hundreds and thousands of cords of wood were hauled from the country east of the Cohansey to those shipping-points and freighted to Philadelphia.

The ring of the woodman's axe was heard all winter long through the forests, and the year around teams, both of oxen and horses, were seen upon all the roads leading from the forests to the river-docks. The people who did all this work were not all Goulds, Pierces, and Murrays, but there were Garrisons, Elmers, Clarks, Woodruffs, Batemans, Lummises, Facemires, Pages, Steelings and hosts of others, whose names are still prominent among their descendants in this county.

Chapter Seven - Origin of the Pierce, Murray, and Cuff Families

Tradition says that the Pierces originated from two mulattoes who were brought here in a vessel from the West Indies, with which the Colony had early trade, vessels from the West Indies arriving at Greenwich and also coming up as far as to what is now Bridgeton. These two men were Richard and Anthony Pierce, brothers. It was the custom in those early days for the landowners to pay the passage of immigrants who came to this country and were unable themselves to pay, and those immigrants would be indentured to the landowners for a term of years, or if they were females, the landowners might make wives of them. [8]

Anthony and Richard Pierce paid the passage of two Dutch women, sisters, from Holland; their names were Marie and Hannah Van Aca. The last name speedily degenerated into Wanaca, and was made the Christian name of a son of one of them. From these descended all the Pierces of Gouldtown. They came to the colony of West New Jersey before the middle of the eighteenth century.

The Murrays originated in Cape May; they claim an Indian ancestry. The first Murray of whom there is trace in the vicinity of the earliest settlements of Gouldtown, was Othniel Murray. He claimed to be a Lenapee or Siconessee Indian, and came from Cape May County. The Lenapees resided in the locality of Cohansey (or Bridgeton) and had quite a settlement at what became known as the Indian Fields, at a run still known as the Indian Field Run. This Othniel Murray married Katharine (last name unknown), a Swede. They had five children, three sons and two daughters, Mark Murray, David Murray, and John Murray, and Mary Murray and Dorcas Murray. From these descended all the Murrays of Gouldtown.

We have now outlined the three chief families of Gouldtown, viz.: Benjamin Gould and Ann, his wife (they had Elizabeth and Benjamin, Jr., who died young). Their other children were Sarah, Anthony, Samuel, Abijah, and Elisha; Sarah died unmarried. Anthony Pierce and Marie (Mary) had many children; their sons were Menon Pierce, Richard Pierce, Anthony Pierce, Jr., Jesse Pierce, 1st, John Pierce, Benjamin Pierce, and Wanaca Pierce, and two daughters, Hannah Pierce and Elizabeth Pierce. Richard Pierce, Sr., and Hannah, had but one son, Adam Pierce, but they had four daughters, viz.: Mary, Rhumah, Hannah, and Elizabeth.

These four families — the children of Benjamin and Ann Gould, the children of Anthony and Mary Van Aca Pierce, the children of Richard and Hannah Van Aca Pierce, and the children of Othniel and Katharine Murray, rapidly intermarried before the Revolution. They also intermarried with white people.

Benjamin Gould's oldest son, Anthony Gould, married Phoebe Lummis, a white girl — one of the Lummises, before named. Her father is believed to have been James Lummis. Benjamin Gould's second son, Samuel Gould, married Rhumah Pierce, daughter of Richard and Hannah Pierce. Benjamin Gould's third son, Abijah Gould, married Hannah Pierce, daughter of Richard and Hannah Pierce. Anthony Pierce's daughter, Elizabeth Pierce, married Josiah Hicks, of Gloucester. Benjamin Gould's fourth son, Elisha Gould, married Elizabeth Pierce, daughter of Richard and Hannah Pierce. Hannah Pierce, born in 1767, married Reuben Cuff, of Salem, the minister. These all lived in colonial times; Adam Pierce, the only son of Richard and Haimah Pierce, and Richard Pierce, Jr., and Anthony Pierce, Jr., served in the Revolutionary War; they were Revolutionary pensioners until their deaths, between 1836 and 1850, at a great age.

One of the sons of Othniel Murray and Katharine, his wife, was also a soldier of the Revolution and was a deserter. It is told of him that an officer from General Joseph Bloomfield's command came after him, and he refused to go. The officer drew his sword and said: "I demand for the last time that you go with me and return to your company; will you go?" Young Murray saw determination in the officer's attitude and he reluctantly replied, "I will go." He returned to the army and served till the end of the war.

Wanaca Pierce, son of Anthony and Mary Van Aca Pierce, married Mary Murray, daughter of Othniel and Katharine Murray. Adam Pierce, son of Richard and Hannah Van Aca Pierce, married Mary Murray's sister, Dorcas Murray.

In the early days the settlements, Gouldtown and Piercetown, were somewhat like those of the Jews and Samaritans about which we read in the New Testament. Each settlement had its own church, its own schoolhouse, and its own family and social customs. The differences in appearance, in manners, in pronunciation and in their general habits and views were marked; and there was no small degree of antipathy or at least mutual disregard existing between the two races. Happily, with the blending of the schools and the general advance of intelligence, much of this mutual disregard has passed away and the people are now much nearer unification.

Not to go at length into particulars, we may remark that in the early times the Pierces exhibited greater fondness for flowers, for bright colors in dress, and for music than did the Goulds. They cared less for home, were more given to hunting and fishing and evinced greater love for amusement. While among the Pierces the old time "fiddle" survived and frolics were held in some far-away cabin of a home where men and women performed some kind of dance, during the same period there was not a musical instrument or musician among the Goulds. It is doubtful if there was a Gould of Gouldtown who could dance a step. Many of the Pierces also had fine musical voices and good ear for music, while the Goulds were markedly defective in both respects.

The Pierces were more devoted to working in the woods and in the marshes, caring less for farming; while the Goulds in the earliest times manifested strong interest towards farming, raising hogs and securing good horses. In manners the Goulds were usually brusque or blunt; the Pierces suave and plausible.

There was a stronger belief in signs, in ghosts, in witches and "conjurors" among the Pierces than among the Goulds, to be traced to their Dutch origin in part; the Goulds, however, were not entirely free from these superstitions. But the great regard for the moon and the deviation of the wind in relation to sowing and planting was usually found coupled more with the Pierce or Murray element of the population than with the Gould.

The Pierces and Murrays had more of the elements which go to make musicians, poets, orators, and singers, than the Goulds. The congregation which assembled in Piercetown, a century or more ago, would produce much better singing and was much more eloquent in speech and prayer than the congregation in Gouldtown. The older Pierces and Murrays could sing, making melody with their voices, while the older Goulds could not. Indeed one of the earliest circuit preachers who came to Gouldtown reported that there was not a man there who could sing "Praise God from whom all blessings flow!"

The Goulds ranked well in sturdy and steady-going ways. They knew how to work from year's end to year's end. They were persevering and frugal, with a commendable zeal for learning. What they lacked of the showy talents they more than compensated for in the homely virtues.

The Goulds of the early generations, as well as the Murrays, were fair-skinned, with blue eyes and light hair. The Pierces were darker complexioned with black hair and black eyes. The young women were noted for their good looks and regular features. The Cuff family origin will be given later. It properly belongs to Salem County.

[8] Professor Kalm, writing from Rancocas, N. J., December 18, 1743, relative to the powers of a clergyman respecting the performance of the marriage ceremony, said: "He cannot marry such strangers as have bound themselves to serve a certain number of years in order to pay their passage from Europe, without the consent of their masters." — New Jersey Archives.

Chapter Eight - Importance of Genealogical Research; Some of the Original Family Genealogies of Salem and Cumberland Counties; Compilation of Thomas Shourds

The "Magazine of American History" says: "The growing interest in ancestry indicates that Americans are fast coming to believe that it is of some consequence to know from whom they are descended. Long lines of ancestry are revealed in every person. Pride in ancestry deserves encouragement. One cannot know too much about himself. Genealogy is the most fascinating branch of history."

The late Thomas Shom'ds, historian of Salem County, nearly forty years ago compiled a long line of Salem and Cumberland County genealogy, which well deserves to be put in permanent form. With that end in view, a portion is given here, which relates to some of the most prominent families in Cumberland County. It embraces the Sheppard family, from which came the first Mayor of Bridgeton, the Bacons of Bacon's Neck, the Wheatons of Greenwich, the Mulfords, the Batemans, the Holmeses, and many more. He wrote:

The Sheppard family is the most numerous of any, excepting the Thompsons, in the ancient County of Salem. There were three brothers, David, Thomas and John Sheppard; they came from Tipperary, Ireland. On their arrival in America they resided for a short time at Shrewsbury, East Jersey. In 1683 they settled in what is now Cumberland County, on the south side of the Cohansey, it being a neck of land bounded on the north by the Cohansey River, on the south by a small creek, called Back Creek. It is not improbable that they gave it the name of Shrewsbury Neck, after the township in East Jersey where they first settled. The Sheppard family, I have no doubt, were English; their name implies as much. The Sheppards were members of the Baptist Church of Cleagh Keaton, in the County of Tipperary, Ireland. They were also among the few persons that organized the First Cohansey Baptist Church, in 1690, at Shrewsbury Neck. David Sheppard's first purchase was fifty acres of land of Captain William Dare; he afterward purchased one hundred and fifty acres, on which he lived and died. I have no doubt he became the owner of a large quantity of land in the Neck.

The Sheppard, Westcott and Reeves families, during the last (eighteenth) century and the fore part of the present (nineteenth), were the principal owners of Back and Shrewsbury Neck. David Sheppard, Sr., agreeably to the most authentic account, had six children: David, born 1690; John, Joseph, Enoch, Hannah, and Elizabeth Sheppard. Hannah married a young man named Gillman. She died in

1722, leaving one son, David Gillman. John, the son of David Sheppard, Sr., died about the year 1719, without issue, leaving his property to his brothers and sisters. David, the eldest son of David Sheppard, the emigrant, was born about the year 1690, and inherited the homestead property of his father, in Back Neck. He married in 1719. The children of David Sheppard, Jr., and his wife, Sarah Sheppard, were Philip, born 1720; Ephraim, born 1722; David, 1724; Joseph, 1727, and Phoebe Sheppard. Philip, the eldest, inherited a large landed estate in Back Neck, on which he resided. The property is now owned by one of the heirs of the late Ephraim Mulford. Philip was twice married; his first wife was Mary, his second Sarah Bennett. He was considered one of the largest and most successful farmers in that neighborhood. Tradition has it that he was the first, in that section, that owned a covered wagon. I do not suppose that it was an elliptic spring carriage, but plain as it was, I have no doubt it was considered by the inhabitants a great innovation. It was then the custom to travel on horseback. Philip died January 5, 1797, aged seventy-seven, leaving a large real and personal estate to his children. His widow, Sarah Sheppard, married John Remington, in 1801. Philip was buried in the Baptist cemetery, near Sheppard's mill; he was a deacon in the church, and was considered one of the most prominent citizens in that section of Cumberland County. The inventory of his personal property at the time of his death amounted to £580 6s. His children by his first wife, Mary, were Amos, Hannah, Mary and Naomi Sheppard. By his second wife, Sarah B. Sheppard, Ichabod, Henry, Phoebe, and William Sheppard. Ephraim, the son of David Sheppard, Jr., born 1722, was married three times. His first wife was Kesiah Kelsey; his second was Sarah Dennis; third, Rebecca Barrett. He lived in Hopewell Township, on the road from Bowentown to Readstown, and was owner of a large landed estate in that section, leaving at his death large farms to all four of his sons, all adjoining one another on the straight road from Bridgeton to Readstown. He was a highly respected citizen, and like his brother Philip, was one of the deacons of Cohansey church. He died May 8, 1783, aged sixty years, and was buried in the Baptist yard adjoining the church, near Sheppard's mill, by the side of his wife, Sarah Dennis, who died 1st mo. 21st, 1777. She died in her fifty-first year. His third wife, Rebecca Barrett, survived him twenty years. She was buried at Shiloh, being a Seventhday Baptist. Ephraim had ten children, all by his second wife, Sarah Dennis. The oldest was Joel, born 1748, Abner, born May, 1750; James, born December 25, 1752; Hannah, and Rachel. Phoebe married Wade Barker, who was the grandson of Samuel Wade, Jr., of Alloway's Creek. She died young, leaving no issue. Wade was buried in the old Baptist yard at Mill Hollow, near Salem. Sarah, Elizabeth, and Hope Sheppard, who afterward married Reuel Sayres, were the other children. Sayres subsequently moved to the State of Ohio. Ephraim's youngest child was Ephraim Sheppard. David, the son of David Sheppard, Jr., was born in the year 1724. He married Temperance Sheppard, daughter of Jonadab and Phoebe Sheppard. They lived in the Township of Downe, Cumberland County. He was a member of Cohansey church, as was also his wife, and both became constituent members of the Dividing Creek Baptist Church at its constitution, May 30, 1761; at that time he became deacon of the church and afterward a colleague of the pastor, Samuel Heaton. David Sheppard died June 18, 1774, aged fifty years; his widow subsequently married a man by the name of Lore. She was born in 1731 and died July 28, 1796, aged sixty-five years; she and her first husband, David Sheppard, were buried at Dividing Creek Baptist graveyard. The following are the names of David and Temperance Sheppard's children; Hosea, David, Owen, Jonadab, Tabitha, Temperance and Mary Sheppard. Joseph the son of David Sheppard, Jr., was born in 1727; he married a Say re. They lived in Back Neck and owned a large quantity of good land, which he left to his children.

I have been informed that most, if not all, of said land has now passed out of their possession. He also left a large personal estate for that time, amounting to £647 12s. He and his wife were members of the Cohansey church. It seems he was a prominent man in that section. He was chosen December 22, 1774, one of the committee of safety for the County of Cumberland, to carry into effect the resolution of the Continental Congress, and on whose hands rested the supreme authority after the war commenced, until the formation of the new State Government gave an organized power in New Jersey. He died 1st mo. 8th, 1782, aged fifty-four years, and was buried on his own farm in an old family burying ground, now long disused. His wife, Mary Sayres Sheppard, was buried in the same yard. She died in 1819, aged fifty-eight years; their daughter, Lydia, also lies there; all three of them have tombstones at the head of their graves. This family graveyard is an exception to the general rule. It was the practice in the early settlement of Fenwick's colony, to have family burying grounds, but the plough has passed over nearly all of them, so no man knoweth where many of our ancestors lay. I have been informed that the ancient Swedish family, the Sinnicksons, cleared their old family graveyard during last year, in Obisquahasett, and their intentions are to keep it in good order — a noble deed. Dr. George B. Wood has likewise recently caused to be erected a monument to his great-grandfather, Richard Wood, who died in 1759, in the family graveyard in Stoe Creek Township, County of Cumberland. Joseph Sheppard, the year before his death, built a large brick house on his property, and died soon afterwards; the house is still standing, and the place is now owned by that enterprising citizen, Richard Laning, the son of John Laning. The following are the names of Joseph Sheppard's children: David, born 1758; Lydia, 1760; Ruth, Isaac, Mary, and Lucy Sheppard.

Lucy, the daughter of Joseph and Mary Sheppard, born November, 1773, married Isaac, son of Isaac and Judith Wheaton, in 1792; Isaac was born September, 1769. By that connection there were seven children — Joseph, the eldest, born in 1795, died March 3, 1871, never married. Their second son, Providence Ludlam Wheaton, born April 21, 1798, died 3d mo. 1st, 1867 — his wife was Ruth Foster — they had one son, Andrew Evan Wheaton, who resides at Greenwich with his mother, Mary Sheppard Wheaton. The eldest daughter of Isaac and Lucy S. Wheaton was born November 20, 1799; she was the second wife of Henry Mulford. Their three oldest children were Anna Maria, Hannah, and Isaac W. Mulford. William Wheaton, the son of Isaac and Lucy Wheaton, was born April 18, 1801, is living in Hopewell Township, and has a large family of children. Isaac Wheaton born February 26, 1803, died July 6, 1846, leaving no children. Hannah, the daughter of Isaac and Lucy S. Wheaton, born in 1805, married in 1823 Gabriel Davis Hall, of Bacon's Neck, son of Ebenezer Hall. Gabriel and his wife had several children. She died August 31, 1849. Amos, the son of Philip Sheppard, born about 1750, subsequently married Hannah Westcott, and died in 1788, at middle age; his widow married John Mulford. Josiah, the eldest son of Amos and Hannah W. Sheppard, born September 14, 1778, his wife was Charlotte Westcott, daughter of Henry and Jane Harris Westcott. He died October 4, 1850. His son, Henry, was born June 3, 1808, married and lives in Stone Creek Township, near Jericho; they have a family of children. Jane, the daughter of Josiah, born in 1811 and died a young woman in 1828. Hannah, the daughter of Josiah and Charlotte W. Sheppard, bora 10th mo. 23rd, 1813, married Ephraim Glaspey; they have a family of children, and reside near the city of Bridgeton. Harriet, the fourth child of Josiah and Charlotte W. Sheppard, born February 19, 1816, married James Sheppard Kelsay in 1837; they have seven children. Martha, the daughter of Amos and Hannah W. Sheppard, born in 1780, subsequently married Charles Westcott, of Sayre's Neck, Cumberland County. She and her husband afterward moved to Covington, Kentucky, where she died in the winter of 1868, having children. Hannah, daughter of Philip and Mary Sheppard, married Ephraim Shaw; they had three children, Harvey, Mary and Lydia. Lydia, the youngest, in 1810, married Henry Whitaker. They reside at Millville and have a large family of children, most of whom are married. Mary, daughter of Philip and Mary Sheppard, never married, and died May 17, 1799, aged about fifty years.

Naomi, daughter of Philip, married William Conner; they had three children, Abigail, the eldest, born August 31, 1754, married Thomas Brooks in 1789; they had ten children. Thomas died September, 1829, and his widow, Abigail Brooks, died August 19, 1841, aged seventy-seven years. Prudence, born 1766, whose first husband was James Sheppard, son of Elias and Susanna Sheppard (James was a nephew of Mark Sheppard, who was one of the first of the Sheppard family that became a member of the Society of Friends). Prudence had one child by her first husband, James Sheppard, which died in infancy. Her second husband was William Johnson, William and Prudence Johnson had eight children. She died 9th mo. 5th, 1869; her last husband, William Johnson, died 2nd mo. 17th, 1831. Ichabod, son of Philip and Sarah Bennett Sheppard, born December 11, 1769, married Ruth Sheppard, daughter of Joel and Hannah Jenkins Sheppard (Joel was a cousin to Ichabod, being the son of Ephraim Sheppard). Ichabod and his wife had two children, Phoebe and Naomi. Ichabod died April 22, 1799, and his widow, Ruth Sheppard, married David Bateman, a minister in the Baptist denomination; they had three sons, Isaac, Daniel and David Bateman. Ruth, their mother, departed this life July 29, 1806. Soon after that event, David Bateman and his three sons, Isaac, Daniel and David, removed to Ohio. Phoebe, daughter of Ichabod and Ruth Sheppard, married on March 28, 1819, John Reeves. There were two children by that connection — one daughter living at this time in the city of Bridgeton, and a son residing near Shiloh. Naomi, second daughter of Ichabod and Ruth Sheppard, born September 17, 1800, and in 1817 she married Jonathan Young, who was afterward drowned at sea; they had five children, all of whom died young, excepting Lewis Young, who is a resident of Bridgeton and was the old Court Crier.

Harvey, son of Philip and Sarah B. Sheppard, married in 1797 Hannah Smith of Greenwich, daughter of Isaac and Cynthia Smith; he had one daughter, Hannah, by his first marriage. She married in 1818 John Test, the son of Francis Test, Jr. John and his second wife, Hannah S. Test, removed to Indiana. He studied law, and was elected to Congress during Andrew Jackson's administration. He was an uncle to Joseph Test, who resides in Salem. The wife of Harvey Sheppard, 2d, was Ruth Ogden, daughter of Elmer and Charlotte Ogden, of Fairfield Township; they had three children, Philip, Abbie and Ruth. The wife of Harvey Sheppard, 3rd, was Amelia Davis, of Shiloh; he and his last wife went West in 1818. Phoebe, daughter of Philip Sheppard, married Joseph Newcomb, they lived in Back Neck, and had two children, Joseph and Sarah S. Newcomb. William, son of Philip Sheppard, born November 29, 1778, married in 1802 Matilda Westcott, daughter of Henry and Jane Harris Westcott; they had six children, Ichabod, William, Sarah, Harris, Phoebe, and Elmer Ogden Sheppard.

Joel, son of Ephraim and Sarah Dennis Sheppard, born in 1748, married Hannah Jenkins, who was born in 1749 and died in 1807; she left seven children, Dennis, Ruth, Sarah, Lydia, Amy, Elizabeth and Reuben Sheppard. Joel's second wife was Letitia Platts, widow of David Platts and daughter of David Gillman; they had no issue. His third wife was Sarah Davis, of Shiloh; they had no children. Joel was a deacon in the old Cohansey Church, and was a large farmer, living in Hopewell Township, and was a prominent citizen. Dennis, son of Joel and Hannah Sheppard, married a young woman by the name of Ayres. They moved to one of the Western States in 1817. Ruth, daughter of Joel Sheppard, married Ichabod, son of Philip and a cousin of her father. Sarah, daughter of Joel and Hannah J. Sheppard, born 1774, married in 1799 Samuel Bond Davis, son of Elnathan and Susanna Bond Davis. Elnathan was the greatest surveyor in his generation in this section of the State for many years after the Revolution. The late Josiah Harrison, of Salem, who died aged over ninety years, who was a surveyor in his early life, told me a short time previous to his death that he regarded Elnathan Davis as captain general of the surveyors of Salem and Cumberland Counties. Samuel B. and Sarah Davis had several children, one of whom, Jarmin A. Davis, lives in Shiloh, and is a Justice of the Peace. Lydia Sheppard, daughter of Joel, married in 1804 Oswell Ayres; they had children but they are all deceased. Amy, daughter of Joel and Hannah Sheppard, born February 15, 1780, in 1803 married Oliver Harris, son of Robert Harris. Oliver and Amy Harris had four children — Hosea, Hannah S., Mary, and Eliza. The latter was born October 14, 1808, and in 1826 married Hezekiah Johnson; they moved to Oregon and are still living. One of their children is Franklin Johnson, D.D., pastor of a Baptist church at Newark, N. J. He is the author of several commentaries on the International Sunday school Lessons, now in general use. Samuel, another son of Oliver and Amy Harris, born November 24, 1813. Elizabeth, daughter of Joel and Hannah Sheppard, in 1805 married Eli Beveman. Soon after their marriage, they moved to Highland County, Ohio; they had issue. Reuben, son of Joel and Hannah Sheppard, married Elizabeth W. Dare, Reuben and his wife moved to Ohio in 1817; they had one son, William Alfred Sheppard, who was a physician at New Vienna, Clinton County, Ohio. He died in 1871, leaving children; Henry A. Sheppard is a lawyer at Hillsboro, Ohio; Abner, second son of Ephraim and Sarah Dennis Sheppard, born May 28, 1750; his first wife was Mary Dowdney, who died about fifteen months after their marriage, leaving one child. Abner's second wife was Ruth Paullin; she died 1797. His third wife was Mary McGear, widow of John McGear; she died in 1809, and his fourth wife was Elizabeth Fithian. Abner was a farmer, and lived in

Hopewell township the greater part of his life. At the time of the American Revolution he was in the militia, and was in Colonel Hand's regiment at the fight of Quinton's Bridge and took part in the battle; he died March 2, 1824. The following are the names of his children: Mary, Ephraim (who died young), Henry, Temperance, Phoebe, Prudence, Delanah, Lafayette, Ruth, Mary, and Ephraim Elmer Sheppard. James Sheppard, the son of Ephraim and Sarah Dennis Sheppard, was born December 25, 1752. His first wife was Hannah Brooks, whom he married January 23, 1774; she died in 1777. His second wife was Keziah Barber; they were married in 1778, She died June 11, 1824 and James, her husband, June 3, 1825. He was a deacon in Cohansey Baptist Church, a farmer and a large landowner in Hopewell Township, and had an excellent character for uprightness in his dealings with his fellowmen, and was greatly respected by all who knew him. He had eleven children.

The children of James and Hannah B. Sheppard were David and Phoebe Sheppard, and by his second wife, Keziah Barber Sheppard, Hannah, Rachel, Mary, Joseph, William, Prudence, Rebecca and Phoebe. Most of those children lived to grow up and marry. William, the son of James Sheppard, born July, 1785, married, March 3, 1808, Ann Husted, daughter of Henry and Ann Sheppard Husted, of Shrewsbury Neck. William was an ordained minister of the Baptist denomination, but never had charge of a church. He was a farmer, and preached as he had opportunity. They had thirteen children. Hannah, the daughter of Ephraim and Sarah Sheppard, born about 1754, married Daniel Moore; she died in 1784. Rachel, another daughter, born in 1761, married James Sayre, who was wounded at the massacre at Hancock's Bridge in 1778. Ephraim, son of Ephraim and Sarah, moved to Salem, and married Elizabeth, widow of John Challis, and mother of John and James Challis; (the latter afterward became an ordained minister among the Baptists). Elizabeth Milbank, mother of these children, was born at Waltham, England, May 2, 1770. Ephraim and his wife, Elizabeth M. Sheppard, had one daughter, Mary W., born in 1809.

David, son of Joseph and Mary Sheppard, born 1758, married in 1783, Phoebe, daughter of Providence and Sarah Ludlam; she died in 1799, leaving six children. Sarah, the eldest child, married in 1803, William S. Walker, a resident of Upper Alloway's Creek, Salem County; they had three children. Phoebe Walker, their eldest daughter, married Thomas Bilderback, of Allowaystown; they left children. William Sheppard, a son, married Ann Stow, and lived on the homestead farm until his death; since that event his widow and his daughters have resided in Salem. Charles H. Walker owns and resides upon the homestead farm.

Joseph, the son of David and Phoebe L. Sheppard, born January 9, 1786, was elected pastor of the First Baptist Church at Salem, in 1809, and was pastor of said church until 1829, and then removed to Mount Holly, where he continued as pastor seven years, but his health failing him, he resigned his pastoral charge and moved to Camden. He never took another pastoral charge, but preached occasionally when health permitted; he died in Camden in 1838, in the fifty-second year of his age. His wife was Hannah F. Budd; they had four children, Mary, Phoebe Ann, Hannah and Josephine Sheppard; they all married but Hannah. Phoebe Ann lived in the State of Georgia. Josephine lived in Washington, D. C, but died about two months since. David Sheppard's second wife was Miriam Smith, widow of Isaac Smith; she died in 1815, and David in 1827. He was a deacon of Cohansey Church, and was a prominent citizen. For many years he lived on the homestead farm in Fairfield Township, but in later years he moved to Bridgeton, and built a large brick mansion on the west side of Cohansey, where his son, Isaac A. Sheppard, lived and died. The dwelling is now known as Ivy Hall Seminary for ladies. Providence Ludlam, son of David Sheppard, born February 21, 1788, married Mary Letson, of New Brunswick, New Jersey. One of their children, Ebenezer L. Sheppard, lives in Pittsgrove Township, and is a member and clerk of the Pittsgrove Baptist Church. He has recently written and published a historical sketch of that church. William and David Ludlam were twin sons of David Sheppard, and were born June, 1790. William died in 1823 and never married. David, his brother, studied for a physician, but died suddenly about the time he was ready to commence the practice of his profession. Ercurious, the son of David, married Martha Lupadius, of New Brunswick. She is still living, but Ercurious is deceased. He left two children, Mary and Martha. Ebenezer, the son of David, born July 23, 1798, died June, 1814. Mary, the daughter of David and Miriam Sheppard, his second wife, married in 1824 Jonathan J. Haun; they had two children, Maria and Mary Haun. The latter married Joseph Moore, homoeopathic physician, of Bridgeton; she died in 1860. Isaac A. Sheppard, son of David, born in 1806, married, 1st of April, 1828, Jane H. Bennett; she died 1839, aged thirty-five years. Isaac's second wife was Hannah B. McLean, whom he married in 1841, but she only lived a little over a year. His third wife was Margaret E. Little, who is still living; they were married in 1850. Isaac A. Sheppard died suddenly in his office in 1863, having been found sitting dead in his chair. He was a deacon of the First Baptist Church of Bridgeton. His oldest son, Isaac A., born in 1829, died April 11, 1832. Jane B., daughter of Isaac A. Sheppard, born in 1821, married, in 1868, Horatio J. Mulford, the eldest son of the late Henry Mulford, of Bridgeton. Horatio, with his brother, Isaac W., and his sisters, were the originators and principal benefactors of the South Jersey Institute, a school for both sexes, located in Bridgeton. The cost of the building has been estimated at $60,000. It has a fine corps of teachers, and has been in operation four years, during which time it has established a reputation equal to the best educational institutions in the country. Horatio's wife, Jane Mulford, like her father, died suddenly, and was found dead sitting in her chair, on the evening of February 9, 1874. She was a woman of great usefulness in the church and in the community, and her loss was deeply felt by all. She left one child, a son, Horatio Jones Mulford, born 1869. There were eight other children of Isaac A. Sheppard's, Miriam, Theodore, Francis, Charles, Elizabeth, Frank, Frederick, and Lillian, widow of Mayor Smalley.

Isaac, son of Joseph and Mary Sheppard, born in 1776, married Sarah, daughter of Jeremiah Bennett; she died in 1797. Isaac's second wife was Jane Harris Westcott, the widow of Henry Westcott, and daughter of Ephraim and Jane Harris, of Fairfield Township, His third wife was Abigail B. Husted, widow of Henry Husted, and daughter of Ichabod Bishop. Isaac Sheppard died December 16, 1815. He had five children: Isaac, the eldest, never married; Henry, the second son of Isaac and Sarah Sheppard, married, March 27, 1811, Eunice Westcott. Soon after their marriage they moved to one of the Western States, and Henry died there. His widow returned to her native State and died in 1868. They had a family of children. Sarah, daughter of Isaac and Sarah Sheppard, born November 23, 1797, married, March 17, 1819, Elmer Ogden; they live in Greenwich, and have several children. Ephraim, the son of Isaac and Jane H. Sheppard, born August 15, 1801, married, in 1819, Jane, daughter of Jehiel and Mary Westcott; she died in 1823. His second wife was Mary, daughter of John and Mary B. Westcott, of Fairfield; she died in 1842, and Ephraim Sheppard died July 9, 1848. His children by his first wife were Ephraim, the eldest, who went West, and died there; and Ehas Sheppard, who died young. Mary Jane, daughter of Ephraim and Mary Sheppard, married Charles Campbell. Isaac Alpine Sheppard, son of Ephraim and Mary Sheppard, went to Philadelphia to live, and subsequently was elected a member of the Pennsylvania Legislature for several sessions. Isaac is the head of the great stove firm of J. A. Sheppard & Company. Joseph, the son of Ephraim Sheppard, married Sarah Flanagan, of Sculltown; they now live in Camden County, between Haddonfield and Camden. Henry, son of Abner and Ruth Sheppard, was born in 1787, and married, the first of December, 1815, Margaret Lummis; she died in 1817. Henry's second wife was Sarah B. Ogden, widow of John B. Ogden. They were married in March, 1819; she died in 1858, and her husband, Henry Sheppard, in July, 1867. He was a hatter, and followed the business many years in Bridgeton, where he settled early in life. He was postmaster for several years in that town. All his children were by his second wife, Sarah B. Ogden. Jane Buck, daughter of Henry and Sarah B. Sheppard, born December 11, 1819, married in 1840, to Lorenzo Fisler Lee; he died July 17, 1848, leaving a widow and four children. Henry Sheppard, Jr., born November 8, 1821, married April 3, 1845, Rhoda S. Nixon, daughter of Jeremiah Nixon. A short time after their marriage they moved to Springfield, Green County, Missouri; and he has prospered there. For many years he and his brother, Charles, did the leading mercantile business of the place, but both have now retired from active business. Henry commanded one of the regiments of the militia of the State and was out several times during the Rebellion. That part of the State suffered much from the war. They have six children, Francis, Henry, John Nixon, Mary Thompson and Margaret Sheppard. Charles, son of Henry and Sarah Sheppard, born September 5, 1823, married November 5, 1856, Lucy Dow, daughter of Ira and Mary Dow, of East Hardwick, Vermont. Charles and his family are living at Springfield, Mo.; he being cashier of Green County National Bank. There are three more children of Henry Sheppard, Sr., Sarah, Margaret, and Joseph Ogden, who I believe reside in Bridgeton. Joseph is a physician, and during the Rebellion for a time served as a surgeon in the army. Ephraim Elmer, son of Abner and Mary Sheppard, born October 2, 1804, married in May, 1828, Jane Elizabeth Dare, daughter of David and Rebecca Fithian Dare. They resided near Bridgeton. Ephraim was elected Clerk of the County of Cumberland in 1852, and served to 1857. He was appointed a Judge of the Court of Common Pleas for said County in 1853, and reappointed in 1868, and was elected Mayor of Bridgeton in the spring of 1873. His term expired in 1876. Ephraim and his wife had eight children. Ephraim Elmer, Jr., born March 19, 1830, married in April, 1856, Lindervilla Maxon Bonham, daughter of Hezekiah Bonham, of Shiloh. They have had seven children, four of whom are living. They reside at Elmer, Salem County. Elizabeth R. Sheppard, born April 6, 1832, married in 1850 George W. Elwell. They live in Bridgeton, and have one son, Albert Sheppard, born March 17, 1853, who is a druggist in Philadelphia. Ruth N. Sheppard, daughter of Ephraim, born December 21, 1834, is not married. David Dare Sheppard, son of Ephraim, born 1836, married October 18, Cornelia Albertson, daughter of Amos Buzby, of Pilesgrove. He was in the dry goods business in Bridgeton until 1870, when he moved to Springfield, Mo., and went into business with his brother, William Sheppard.

John Caldwell Calhoun, son of Ephraim Sheppard, born in 1840, married in 1861, Jane Elizabeth Smith, of Philadelphia, and resides in that city.

William E. Sheppard, son of Ephraim, born February 28, 1842, married, March 18, 1869, Josephine M. Trull, daughter of Nathaniel Trull, of North Tewksbury, Mass. They moved to Springfield, Mo., in the fall of 1866, and he is in business with his brother, David Sheppard.

Enoch Fithian Sheppard, son of Ephraim, born August 21, 1844, died is 1846. Charles E., [9] son of Ephraim and Jane Elizabeth Sheppard, born November 1, 1846. He is a lawyer and resides in Bridgeton.

[9] At this day (1913) nearly everybody in Cumberland County knows Charles E. Sheppard, the lawyer, so prominently connected with the prosecution of violators of the law regarding the sale of intoxicants.

Chapter Nine - Rural Sociological Examples, Suggested in this Life of Simplicity

John Murray, son of Othniel Murray and Katherine Murray, was born in 1751, or twenty-six years before the death of Benjamin Gould, 1st.

His wife, Tabitha Lupton, a white woman, was born in 1763. They lived neighbors to Benjamin and Ann Gould.

John Murray died in 1853, at the age of one hundred and two years, and his wife Tabitha died November, 1859, aged ninety-six years. The writer of this was born in 1840 and is the grandson of Benjamin Gould, 2nd, and great-grandson of Abijah Gould, 1st, and great-great-grandson of Benjamin Gould, 1st.

I have been many a time to the home of John and Tabitha Murray, when a boy; it was but a mile from the home of my great-great-grandfather. I was but thirteen years old at the time of the death of John Murray, and nineteen when Tabitha Murray died. Their great grandson, Eli Gould, became the husband of my sister Mary.

The four sons of Benjamin Gould were associates of John Murray and his brothers and sisters in their boyhood and early manhood days. Elisha Gould, youngest son of Benjamin, was born in 1755, but he died in 1804, aged forty-nine years. The other sons of Benjamin, as well as Sarah, the daughter, were much older than Elisha. Anthony Gould was the oldest; then came Samuel, and Abijah. The sons and daughters of Anthony and Richard Pierce were also companions of the sons of Benjamin Gould.

It is not hard to see how the tradition of Goulds, as well as the Pierces, could be handed down by even John Murray, who lived during the last twenty-six years of Benjamin Gould's life, and well into the early lives of his descendants, as well as those of the Pierces.

As I have related, I have seen John Murray and been to his house many, many times; he was a brusque, eccentric old man, and had had both feet cut off. His farm was infested with sand burrs and working in his fields in his bare feet, he got the burrs in his feet, gangrene ensued, and both of his feet were amputated.

He used to put himself in the third person much when talking and he "swore a little" in his general conversation. In those days surgeons did not use anaesthetics in their operations, and it was related of Murray when Dr. Jonathan Elmer was cutting off his feet, that the patient became impatient and blurted out in anger to the doctor, "Hum, damn, if John had his old saw, I'd 'a' had them legs cut off long ago."

I have myself seen him sitting in his doorway in the sunshine; this was his favorite place when the weather suited him. He would sit there and mark by the shadows cast in the doorway (marking on the bare floor) the ascension and descension of the sun during the seasons; and also note the progression and retrogression of the moon, and the progress of the stars. As a little boy, I thought it a rare treat to go to see "Uncle Johnnie and Aunt Tabitha." She was a gentle, lovable old lady; and while I had heard stories of how "Uncle Johnnie" would fire his crutches across the house at Aunt Tabitha when angry, I never saw anything of the kind.

He, like others of Gouldtown, owned a large body of salt marsh along the bay and river shores, where they would mow and gather the salt hay for their cattle, oxen, and horses, and haul it the ten or twelve miles to their homes.

It was the custom for those of Gouldtown to go upon the marshes on Monday and remain day and night until Saturday, where they would mow "shallop" loads of the salt hay and stack it up to haul home in the winter time.

It was related of John Murray that he would go with his sons and the other men down to the marshes, where all would work in common, helping each other get the hay, each having his own body of marsh. Murray would stay upon the wagons and "load" the hay as the men would pitch it up to him, and when driven up to the stacking place, he would pitch it off the wagon.

One time his ox team was proceeding to the haystack with a load of hay, when a savage bull, roaming over the marsh, made attempt to attack the ox team. The old man seized his pitchfork and hurled it into the animal's flank;

the bull, in torture, dashed away across the marsh, the pitchfork finally falling from the beast. "Hum, damn," his favorite expletive, "Hum, damn, John made him fly!" he cried out to the men in glee.

A study of the rural sociology of the times of this generation would be no less interesting, surely, than their ethnology; in the blood of these was the Celtic, Teutonic, African and Indian, with sundry subdivisions, as shown in the pure English, Dutch, and local admixtures.

The Quaker solidity and quiet dispositions inherited by the Goulds may be traced to this day; the Dutch superstitions are still apparent in the Pierces; and the Indian love of "firewater" has been ever noticeable in the Murrays. The Goulds were never addicted to excessive use of liquor, while the Pierces and Murrays were more liberal in its indulgence.

These branches had all large families; how they managed to support them is an interesting question; and yet they lived in comfort and in happiness, as compared to much that is seen in rural life nowadays. Money was an almost unknown commodity in those days and yet property was accumulated.

Old Stone Church, Fairfield.

Reared in the woods, as we look at it in these days, those people were almost "children of the forest"; they cut down the forests and made their farms; they populated the wilds and made a living. The times from the marriage of Benjamin and Ann Gould, about 1725, to that of their death in 1777, were not as prosperous as they were in localities westward from the Cohansey; the march of population had hardly proceeded from Salem across the Cohansey and northward from New England town; what population there was had been pushed out, as it were, from among those of the early settlers who had been at Greenwich, crossed the Cohansey at that place and stretched outward into Fairfield, Shrewsbury Neck, and about New England town.

There were no schools in Gouldtown yet; there were, however, some sources for getting information; some of the Gould children learned to read and write. Anthony Gould, oldest son of Benjamin Gould, could write — for, to a deed made by him in 1802 for a piece of property he had purchased in 1767, he had signed: "At'ty Gould," abbreviating his name with his own hand.

Fancy a gathering of the young people of the names of Gould, Pierce, Murray, Lummis, Mullica, Gates, Hand, and others, known to have populated that section of territory, and imagine, if possible, their occupations and recreations.

Their nearest church was the "Old Stone Church" at New England crossroads; they went to this church when they went anywhere to meeting, and in its adjoining cemetery some of them were afterward buried; probably they went to "meeting" there once or twice a year. It may have been oftener.

Socially, they met in apple-cuttings, quiltings, and hog killings and beef killings. A favorite gathering with them was the "chopping frolic," where the men would show their prowess in felling and "logging" into cord-wood the primeval trees. These "chopping frolics" were attended with hard cider, or apple-jack drinking; while the wives and sisters of the choppers would gather at the home for whose benefit the chopping was made, have a quilting and spinning party, all to be topped off towards night with a big supper and plenty of doughnuts and pies. I have been told that these wood-choppers would vie with each other to be first at the chopping in the woods in the morning and often by noon the long tiers of wood would be ranked up, and the laughing choppers would wend their way to the homestead, where a substantial dinner would await them. In such cases the afternoon would be given over to sport and "waiting on the women." The boys and young men would have jumping, running and wrestling matches, and have as much of a good time as do the boys of the present day. Such are the pictures which have been handed down by my ancestors. Drunkenness was not countenanced, and the man who got too much apple-jack lost his respectability.

How did these old men support their families? Benjamin Gould with his sons, Anthony, Samuel, Abijah, and Elisha, together with the daughter, Sarah — all these children born between 1730 and 1755, — and the many sons and daughters of Anthony Pierce; Menon, Richard, Jesse, Benjamin, John, Anthony, and Wanaca, together with the two daughters, Hannah and Elizabeth; and the son of Richard Pierce, Adam, and the four daughters, Mary, Rhuniah, Hannah and Elizabeth; and the three sons and two daughters of Othniel Murray: Othniel, Jr., David and John (whose name begins this chapter), and daughters: Mary (Polly) and Dorcas, all born and mostly grown up before the Revolutionary War. Their home life as handed down in oral tradition is a study. The high price of food and clothing may have been felt by them then, as by us now, but a study of their habits and resources does not make it appear so.

Take for instance, the crop-gathering time — the haying before alluded to, when the wife and daughters would bake up the great loaves of rye bread in the ovens, and the huge pies, and boil the "chunks" of fat pork and the big pot of vegetables, and bake the molasses cake with which to put up a supply of food for the men-folks to take to the marsh the next week to last them from Monday to Saturday — but this is all over with, when the time for gathering in the fall crops arrives. The cabbage, potatoes, turnips, apples and pumpkins are gathered and stored; the apples are buried in the apple-hole in the ground; the potatoes and turnips are buried in the same way; the cabbages are put in the cabbage-house; a sort of shack made over an excavation a couple of feet deep, and eight or ten feet long, over which tent-like poles are placed, covered over with cornstalks and trash, and then all covered with earth, making an A-shaped shelter, open at the south end, and tightly closed everywhere else. In this the cabbages are stowed away, the door closed up temporarily, and everything is safe within for winter use. The rye and wheat have been stacked up or put in the barns, to be threshed out with flail in the winter.

The fatted hogs are killed and the supply of pork salted down; a fat beef slaughtered, and the beef "corned"; and the family now has no fear of a shortage of rations during the winter. As for fresh food, the woods abound with deer, squirrels, rabbits, coons, possums, quail, and pheasant, which are shot or trapped, at pleasure. There were no game laws.

Fuel is no object of worry; it is had for the labor of chopping and hauling from their own grounds; and the big fire-place uses up a large quantity during the cold weather. The great back-log, which has been hauled up to the door of the "cottage" — generally a log "cottage" at that — is ready to be put in place; a log chain is extended through the house from front door to back door, a yoke of oxen hitched to one end of the chain while the other end is fastened to the log; skids and round sticks for rollers are placed, and the word given: "Whoa-haw, Buck and Berry, Gee up, gee — whoa!" and the log is hauled by the oxen into the house, where it is now rolled into the back of the great fireplace.

Everything is thus ready for the winter's coming. All that remains to do thereafter is to cut and haul logs and cord-wood to the landings for the spring shipments. Such was mostly the family life of the early inhabitants of Gouldtown. The women folk kept up their portion, in spinning, knitting, and making the garments for the household.

Chapter Ten - Gould Genealogies; Probability of Origin of Name of the Settlement

When Gouldtown was first given its name does not yet definitely appear. It was called "Gouldtown, an ancient settlement" many years ago, and records show that it was called "Gouldtown" when Bridgeton was called "Bridgetown" or "The Bridge"; old records, before 1800, make mention of "on the road from Gouldtown to Bumbridge" — meaning what is now Fairton. A chronicle of the Gould families just before and just following the Revolutionary War discloses good grounds for calling the settlement "Gouldtown" during that period.

The New Jersey archives at Trenton attempt to give the record, among other things, of the marriages in the State in colonial times, and in the times immediately following the close of the war of the Revolution; but the reports are woefully inadequate, or else they are not published in those archives. Among the few dozen marriages recorded from Cumberland County is noted that of Anthony Gould and Phoebe Lummis, dated May 16, 1781. This is the first and only Gould, of Gouldtown, whose marriage is thus recorded.

Anthony Gould must have been well advanced in years at this time — though not an old man. He was the oldest living son of Benjamin and Ann Gould, and their youngest son, Elisha, born in 1755, was twenty-six years old at the time of his brother Anthony's marriage, but Anthony was a man and had bought and owned land at least fourteen years before this, as is to be seen in the record of a deed he made to Jacob Steeling in 1802, the year before his death. This deed was made April 10, 1802, between Anthony Gould and Jacob Steeling, and recites the sale by Gould to Steeling of twenty-eight and a quarter acres of land for $113: "Beginning at a red oak corner standing by the present highway leading from Bridgetown to the Beaver dam or Maurice River bridge; thence...binding on (other) land of Anthony Gould to a black oak corner standing in the line between David Seeley and said Gould...containing twenty-eight and a quarter acres of land, be the same more or less, which lot or piece of land the said Anthony Gould purchased of John Page and Thomas Gentry as by Page's deed, dated the fifth day of November, 1767; as by Gentry's deed dated November the thirtieth day, 1796, recourse thereto being had may more at large appear." Anthony Gould had 34¼ acres besides, which was sold by Jonathan Bowen, his executor.

There is no record of the date of Anthony's birth, but it must have been about 1735, for Benjamin land Ann were married and had two children before Anthony, as has been already shown. Anthony sold this land in 1802; his wife had previously died; he signed the deed by his own hand "At'ty Gould."

He died in 1803, leaving a will which was proved September 27, 1803. He left three daughters, Phoebe, Martha (transcribed in the record in Trenton "Mathila") and Christiana, or "Kitty" as she was known. The settlement was called Gouldtown before this, and as the venerable Judge Elmer, then a lad of ten years, said "is of quite ancient date." Martha was the youngest. Phoebe was over eighteen years old at the time her father made his will, for by his will Jonathan Bowen, who resided at the Beaver Dam, was made guardian for Christiana and Martha only. These girls were very fair, and Phoebe shortly after her father's death went to Philadelphia, where she married a man who became mayor of that city, and she no doubt became the mother of children whose descendants have become distinguished. She, of course, lost her identity. * Christiana married first her cousin, Charles Gould, son of her youngest uncle, Elisha Gould, and they had three sons, Daniel Gould, Aaron Gould, and Anthony Gould, 2nd. Daniel Gould was the oldest, and in early manhood, went to Massachusetts (returning to Gouldtown but once, which was in 1852 or 1853), losing his identity as colored. Aaron was born in 1810, and died in 1894, aged eighty-four years. Anthony was born in 1813 and died in 1891, aged seventy-eight years. After the birth of these three sons, Charles, the husband and father, died; a few years later, the widow, "Kitty," married Furman Gould, another cousin of hers, the son of Abijah Gould, 1st, her father's brother. They had five sons and two daughters. The sons were Jonathan Gould, Furman Gould, Jr., Alfred Gould, Theophilus Gould, and Charles Gould. Theophilus died a young man. Of the daughters, Martha and Christiana, the last is the only one now living and she is nearly ninety years of age.

Tamson Cuff, Daughter of Benjamin and Phoebe Gould

Abijah Gould, Son of Benjamin Gould, and Grandson of Abijah Gould I.

Samuel Gould, the son of the Founder of Gouldtown, married Rhumah, second daughter of Richard and Mary Pierce. They had one son, Samuel, Jr., and two daughters, Hannah, and Anna. Anna became the last wife of Rev. Reuben Cuff. Samuel, Jr., married his cousin, Elizabeth, daughter of his uncle, Elisha, and had one son, Samuel, 3rd. Samuel, 2nd died early in life, and his widow, Elizabeth, married Daniel Siro, son of Simon Siro and Mary Pierce, oldest daughter of Richard and Mary Pierce.

Samuel, 3rd, when a young man, went to Pittsburgh, then counted to be in the far west, and all trace of him was lost. Daniel and Elizabeth Siro had one son, Andrew. Then Daniel died and Elizabeth was again left a widow. Hannah Gould went to Philadelphia, where she married an East India sailor, named Charles Gonzales Smith. They had two children, Ann Smith and another who died an infant, and was buried at Gouldtown. The husband, Smith, was lost at sea. She afterwards became the wife of Thomas Wester.

Andrew Siro went to New Bedford, and became a whaler, making many voyages to the northern seas. He came home annually until 1854, since when nothing was ever heard from him and it is supposed he perished at sea. He never married, so far as known.

Abijah Gould, second son of the founder, married Hannah, born in 1756, the third daughter of Richard and Mary Pierce. They had five sons and one daughter, Sarah; she never married and died a young woman. The sons were Benjamin Gould, 2nd, born in 1779, Richard Gould, born in 1783, Abijah Gould, Jr., Leonard Gould and Furman Gould, the youngest.

Samuel Gould, the third son of the founder, sailed in the privateer schooner, "Governor Livingston," which was built at Cohansey, and sailed in 1780. She made one successful trip, when Gould seems to have tired of the sailor life and left her. On her second trip she was captured by the British.

Benjamin Gould, 2nd, married Phoebe Bowen, of Salem County, who was born in 1788. Their living descendants in 1910 are given in pages succeeding. Their children, nine in number, were Oliver, Tamson, Lydia, Jane, Abijah, Sarah, Rebecca, Phoebe, and Prudence.

Benjamin Gould died in 1851, aged seventy-two years; his widow, Phoebe, died in 1877, aged eighty-nine years. Oliver Gould married Rhuhamah, the daughter of Mordecai Cuff, of Salem. They had a number of children, all of whom are now dead, except one, the youngest son, Abijah, 4th. The oldest son, Benjamin Gould, 3rd, went to Boston when a young man, and nothing was heard from him after the first year or two after he went away. Tamson Gould married William Cox, an Indian half-breed. They resided on a farm in Dutch Neck; and William Cox was the first dairyman to sell milk in Bridgeton. They had three sons, William, Jr., Isaac, and Levi.

William, Jr., ran away and went to sea, and the last ever heard from him was a letter mailed from the Golden Gate, California. Isaac also, after growing up "followed the water" for several years, went to Europe at the outbreak of the Civil War and became a blockade runner, carrying English goods into the Southern States. Levi also went to sea and finally became boatswain on a ship trading between Liverpool and China. He died suddenly on his vessel's deck in Liverpool. His effects were sent home to his mother, then a widow for the second time, and residing in Philadelphia.

William and Tamson Cox had also four daughters, Mary, Hannah, Phoebe, and Caroline; the last died a little girl, and William Cox, the husband and father, died. When the children were all grown, Tamson again married — this time she married Reuben Cuff of Salem, son of the minister; they resided on a large farm in Salem County, and kept a big dairy. Mrs. Cuff was noted for her fine cheeses. This Reuben Cuff died in a few years (they had no children) and Mrs. Cuff removed to Philadelphia, where she became housekeeper for two Quaker women with whom she spent the rest of her life.

Mrs. Lydia Sheppard, Daughter of Benjamin and Phoebe Gould, who Lived to be 102 Years Old, and was the Head of Her Son's Household Till the Last Day of Her Life

She died in 1877, in her own house in Gouldtown, which she had built, her death occurring three days before the death of her mother, which was on May twenty-sixth of that year at the old Gould homestead.

None of Tamson's sons ever married so far as known; the oldest daughter, Mary, married Thomas Almond, a barber, who removed from Philadelphia to Bridgeton, where he carried on the business for several years. He died in Philadelphia; they had two daughters, Caroline and Phoebe (Mrs. White), the latter still living as is also her widowed mother, both residing together in Philadelphia. Caroline is dead, one daughter surviving her. Mrs. White has no children. Hannah Cox married Charles Wilson, of Salem, who engaged in tenant farming, but died in a few years; they had no children. Hannah then married Hiram Cuff, a cousin of her first husband who was also a Salem County farmer, residing as tenant farmer on a three-hundred acre farm for many years; they had no children and Hannah died in 1907.

Phoebe Cox married Thomas W. Almond, of Philadelphia, a relative of her sister Mary's husband; he was an undertaker. He died suddenly and his widow and son, William, succeeded to the business. Phoebe in a few years also died suddenly, and the son, William, and his son, succeeded to the business. William died two years ago, and now his widow and their son succeed to the same undertaking business in Philadelphia.

Lydia Gould, born October 22, 1809, the third daughter of Benjamin and Phoebe Gould, married David Sheppard, of Port Elizabeth; they made their home in Millville. There were born to them Tamson, who married Joseph Wilson of Salem, she died in 1874, age thirty-five, leaving no children; Thomas, still residing in Millville; Sarah, wife of B. F. Pierce of Fairton, and David, born two weeks after his father died. David died about six years ago, aged sixty-two years, leaving no children. Lydia, the mother, died in November, 1911, a short time after she had passed the one hundred and second anniversary of her birth. Thomas has two sons and one daughter. Sarah has six daughters and one son.

Jane Gould married Daniel Webster, and they had many children, all of whom are dead but one son, Charles. The father, Daniel, died many years ago, and the mother, Jane, died in 1868, aged fifty-six years.

Abijah Gould, 3rd, married Emily Gould, daughter of Jesse Gould; they had three children, Elizabeth, Josephine, and Dr. Jesse Gould, of Philadelphia. Abijah died in 1892, aged seventy-seven. His wife had died a few years before.

James Steward. Taken when visiting His Daughter, Mrs. Felts, in Wilmington, Delaware.

Sarah Gould married Abel Lee; they had six children; three daughters and three sons, B. F. Lee (Bishop Lee), William Cox Lee, and Abel Lee. The daughters are Elizabeth, Jane, and Isabel. Abel Lee, the father, died in 1852, his widow, Sarah, died a few years ago, over ninety years of age. Two sons, William and Abel, are dead.

Rebecca Gould, born May 2, 1820, married James Steward in 1838; they also had three sons and three daughters, all still living. They are Margaret, William, Mary, Theophilus, Alice, and Stephen. Rebecca died three weeks after the death of her mother, Phoebe, and sister Tamson, in 1877. Tamson's house was but a few hundred yards from the home of her sister, Rebecca

Steward, while the aged mother's home was nearly two miles from both. Mrs. Steward, dividing her time between the bedside of her mother at one extreme, and that of her sister at the other, was prostrated after the double funeral, and died three weeks after, aged fifty-seven years.

James Steward was a man of sterling character, and of more than average intelligence, as was also his wife. He was a bound boy, indentured to a man named Reeves, in Back Neck, who ill-treated him so much that he ran away from him before he was nine years old, and went to live with Elijah Gould, the father of Rev. Theodore Gould. His parents had gone to Santa Domingo in the Bowyer expedition of 1824, leaving him with Mr. Gould, his only remaining relative here being a little dead sister lying in the Gouldtown graveyard.

It was learned that his parents engaged in coffee growing in Santa Domingo, but in a few years no more was ever heard from them.

James Steward, the husband and father, died in May, 1892, aged seventy-seven years and three days. He was a mechanic and had been employed in the works of the Cumberland Nail and Iron Company fifty-one years. The last thirty-five years he had been foreman of the sheet-iron mill.

Phoebe Gould the next to the youngest daughter, married Nathan Gould, son of Abijah Gould, Jr., 2nd. They resided opposite where is now the reservoir on the Bridgeton and Millville Turnpike, on the farm now owned by George T. Pearce. They had three sons and two daughters. Two sons, Joseph and Clarence, are still living, and Nancy, the youngest daughter, wife of George W. Gould, still lives, residing in Atlantic City. The other daughter, Amanda, wife of Edward Cruise, is dead. The last daughter of Benjamin and Phoebe Gould, Miss Prudence F. Gould, ex-

Mrs. Rebecca Steward, Daughter of Benjamin and Phoebe Gould, Wife of James Steward, and Mother of the Steward Group of Three Sons and Three Daughters.

schoolteacher, and dressmaker for all the neighborhood, beloved by every one, dwells now at the old homestead where she was born, and which she owns — that land bequeathed by Benjamin Gould, 1st, to his son Abijah Gould, 1st, who was the grandfather of Miss Prudence.

Richard Gould, second son of Abijah Gould 1st, married Charlotte Gould, daughter of Elisha Gould. They had five sons and three daughters. Richard Gould was born in 1783 and died in 1855, aged seventy-two years. His wife, Charlotte, was born in 1786 and died in 1876, aged ninety years. Their sons were Norton, Andrew, Elijah, Robert and Richard, Jr. The daughters were Rhumah, Sarah and Hannah. Norton died in 1892, aged seventy-eight years, and left a number of descendants, one of whom is Mrs. Ruth Tudas, of Bridgeton. Andrew Gould left a number of descendants; his two sons, Charles and Robert, reside in Bridgeton. His wife was Ann Smith, daughter of Hannah Gould and Charles Gonzales Smith, the East Indiaman. Robert Gould, the third son, went to Canada, where he resided several years, and afterwards returned to Michigan, where he probably died. Richard, Jr., died in Salem; his wife was Martha Emery of Salem. They left a number of children. Rhumah Gould married John Hammond. They had a number of children, some of whom still survive. Hannah Gould married William Jones. They had no children. Some of John Hammond's and Rhumah's children reside in Bridgeton, and two sons, Charles and Arthur, reside somewhere in the far West; Arthur at Saginaw, Michigan.

Anthony Gould

Furman Gould's children were Jonathan Gould, Furman Gould, Jr., Alfred Gould, Charles Gould, and Theophilus Gould. Furman's first wife, the mother of these boys, and two daughters, Martha and Christiana, was Christiana or "Kitty," the widow of Charles Gould, son of Elisha Gould. Though "Kitty" was the mother of ten children, three by her first husband and seven by Furman, she died in 1841 at the age of thirty-seven years. Furman Gould, Sr., became the first local preacher of Gouldtown. He died in 1855, aged sixty-nine years. His stepchildren were Daniel Gould, who went to Massachusetts, Aaron Gould, and Anthony Gould, 2nd. Aaron Gould married Catherine Pierce, daughter of Wanaca Pierce, 1st. They had four children, Timothy, still living; Thomas, dead; Lydia Ann, the wife of Job Cuff, of Hancock's Bridge, and Aaron Paul, still living. Catherine died in 1887, aged seventy-six years. Aaron died in 1894, aged eighty-four years.

Anthony Gould, 2nd, born in 1813, married Almeda, daughter of Jesse Pierce and Christina Stoms, a Dutch woman from Salem County. (It is said Anthony resembled his grandfather Anthony, 1st.) They left numerous descendants, a grandson being Anthony Pierce, the well-known electrician and foreman of electrical wiring for the Bridgeton and Millville Traction Company. The children of Anthony and Almeda Gould were Phoebe, William, Elizabeth, Christina, Christiana, and Almeda; the oldest, Phoebe, and the youngest, Almeda, still survive; all the others are dead.

Phoebe is now nearing her eightieth birthday. William was a soldier in the war of the Rebellion, and died two years ago. Phoebe married Francis L. Pierce, of Canton, who is dead. They had four daughters, Prudence, wife of Charles H. Pierce, engineer at the Ferracute Machine Works; Marietta, wife of Robert 'Pierce; Dorothy, wife of Rev. Alex. W. Pierce, and Phoebe Jane, wife of Fenwick Wright. These last have a musical family, who unite in orchestral performances by string or wind instruments. The sons of Francis L. and Phoebe Gould Pierce, are Anthony, the electrician, Francis, Jr., a barber, at Bristol, Pa.; Amos, also a barber at Coatesville, Pa., and Harold, a hotel chef, now at Commercial Hotel, Bridgeton.

William Gould married Hannah Caroline Gould, daughter of Elisha Gould, Jr. They had two daughters, Luella, wife of John Coombs, and Melissa, wife of George Cuff, of Salem County. William and his wife are both dead.

Elizabeth Gould married Archibald Cuff, Jr. They have two sons and one daughter living. The sons are Edmund and Reuben, both married, and the daughter is Fanny, wife of Luther D. Gould, a former corporal in the Tenth Cavalry, U. S. Army, who served among the Indians and in Cuba, where he figured in rescuing Colonel Theodore Roosevelt and his Rough Rider regiment of Volunteers at Las Guasimas, Cuba.

Christina Gould married Robert Dunn; they had two daughters, Estella and Almeda. Both Robert Dunn and his wife have passed away. Estella married Rev. Burgoyne Cuff, 2nd. He died early, leaving no children. After the death of her mother, with whom she resided many years after the decease of her father and her husband, Estella married Howard Stewart. They own a farm in Gouldtown upon which they reside, and have no children. Almeda Gould, the other daughter of Robert and Christina Dunn, married Joseph Gould, grandson of Rev. Furman Gould, who resides on the farm where once his grandfather lived. They have several children.

Christiana Gould married Mordecai Pierce, a blacksmith of Canton, N. J. They had two sons, Belford, at present a blacksmith in Bridgeton, and Warner K., a member of the Board of Education of Fairfield Township. Christiana died early, and Mordecai later married Anna, daughter of Jonathan Gould. They had two sons and two daughters, Mordecai, Sylvester, Lucette and Madge. Sylvester, a cigar-maker, died a young man; Mordecai resides in Pennsylvania; Lucette is principal of the Gouldtown public school, and Madge is a student in the Bridgeton High School. Anna, the mother, was the postmistress at Gouldtown until the post-office there was abolished.

The wife of Anthony Gould, 2nd, Almeda, died in 1844, aged thirty-three years. Many years after this he remarried — his oldest daughter, Phoebe, having been his housekeeper all these years, and characterized as the "Little Mother" of the family by the whole neighborhood. Anthony Gould at this time married Harriet Gould Cuff, daughter of Leonard Gould, and widow of Ephraim Cuff. There were born to them Anthony Gould, 3rd, Preston Gould, Harriet, Cynthia, and Ida. Only Preston and Ida survive.

Anthony Gould died in 1891, aged seventy-eight years; Harriet Gould, his widow, in 1895, aged seventy-two years. She left children by her former husband Ephraim Cuff: three sons, Quinton Cuff, Lambert Cuff and Theodore Cuff; the last now dead. Quinton resides in Chester, Pa., and Lambert in Gouldtown.

Furman Gould, Sr., the Furman Gould of whom we have spoken, was something of a blusterer in his early days. During the war of 1812, it is told he, together with a man named David Cams, were chartered to take a four-horse load of commissary stores down to Cape May for the garrison located there. One of the lead horses, belonging to Gould, had the name of "Spaddle Ham" on account of being spotted on his rump. A British ship had got too far in shore at Cape May, where she grounded when the tide went out. As the commissary team was approaching the island, the man-o'-war fired a broadside from her port guns. The shot, of course, went way inland. "By Goose, Dave" (his favorite swear-word), "by Goose, that sounds wus'n thunder," said Gould, with some agitation. Driving on a little further, the ship blazed away with another broadside. This time the shot cut off the tops and branches of trees all around them. "Hold on, Furm; stop, I must get out o' here!" cried out David in terror. "Peddee — whoa, come about here, Spaddle Ham!" yelled Furm to his horses, and with lines and whip he brought the team to a right-about-face; and they tell to this day that Furm Gould and Dave Cams ran their horses from Cape May to Dennisville before they stopped them. Whether this tale is true or not, it is a fact that Furman Gould was given by the United States Government a quarter section of land (160 acres) in the State of Illinois, for serving in the war of 1812. This land was sold in 1855 to Henry Gould, who had gone to Illinois the year before.

Furman Gould, Jr., married Hester Cuff, sister of Jonathan Gould's wife. They had four children, two sons and two daughters. The two sons, Albert and William C. Gould survive; of the two daughters. Prudence, who became the wife of Stephen S. Steward, died in 1890, aged forty-two years; Martha, the second, went to Illinois, with an uncle and aunt, lost her identity of color, married a wealthy farmer, and has an interesting family of distinguished westerners. Furman Gould, Jr., died in 1883 aged sixty-six years; his widow, Hester Gould, passed away in 1893, aged seventy-two years.

Jonathan Gould married Hannah Ann Cuff, the daughter of William Cuff, of Salem, son of Rev. Reuben Cuff. They had three children, Lorenzo F. Gould,

Hannah Ann, wife of Rev. Jeremiah H. Pierce, and Anna Rebecca, wife of Mordecai C. Pierce. These three are all living and have numerous children. Jonathan Gould the father died in 1893, aged seventy-seven; his widow, Hannah Ann, died a few years ago aged over eighty.

Alfred Gould married Sarah, a daughter of Elijah and Hannah Murray Gould. They had three children, Eugene Gould, Mary E. Gould and Alice Gould. Alice died of typhoid fever after graduating from the Second Ward public school, Bridgeton, and teaching school in Gouldtown. She was a young woman of high accomplishment. Eugene and Mary are still living on their old homestead, a rich and beautiful farm, both unmarried, with their widowed mother, now in her ninetieth year. She is a sister of Rev. Theodore Gould, who is long past his eighty-second birthday. Alfred Gould died in 1902, aged eighty years. He was born May 13, 1822.

Charles Gould, the youngest son of Furman Gould, Sr., married Susan, the daughter of Abijah Gould, 2nd. They had a number of children, most of whom still live. Joseph, the second of their sons, resides at the old homestead of his father, which was also the home of his grandfather and a part of the original Gould tract; he is a thrifty farmer, and has an interesting family. His wife was Almeda, daughter of Robert and Christina Gould Dunn. Martha Gould, oldest daughter of Furman and "Kitty" Gould,

Mrs. Sarah Gould, Widow of Alfred Gould and Sister of Rev. Theodore Gould.

married Elmer, oldest son of Abijah Gould, 2nd, and had several children, most of whom are dead. Elmer died in 1866. Furman, 3rd, their son, went West before the war of the Rebellion; lost his identity of color, became a thrifty farmer and at last lost himself to all his people in the East. Christiana Gould, the remaining daughter of Furman Gould, Sr., married Menon Pierce, 3rd, and is still living in Gouldtown. They never had any children. Menon, who was a carpenter, died in (   ). This disposes of the immediate descendants of Furman and "Kitty" Gould; and "Kitty" and Charles Gould.

Abijah Gould, 2nd, married Rachel Hicks, daughter of Josiah Hicks and Elizabeth Pierce; they resided on a part of the patrimony of his father, Abijah Gould, 1st, who had received it by will from Benjamin Gould, 1st. The house was located on the Buckshutem road, and is now owned by Joseph Gould, a grandson of Abijah Gould, 2nd. They had five sons and four daughters. The sons were Elmer, Nathan, Mason Mulford, Joseph and Moses; the daughters were Elizabeth, Maria, Susan and Caroline.

Elmer married Martha Gould (as shown on another page). Elizabeth (Betsy), married Adam Pierce, 3rd, and Maria married Smith Gould, as has been also shown, and Caroline, the youngest, married Timothy Gould, son of Aaron Gould. Caroline is dead, but her husband survives. They had two sons and two daughters, who are still living here. Susan married Charles Gould, as appears on another page. Nathan Gould married Phoebe, daughter of Benjamin Gould, 2nd; they are both dead, but two sons and one daughter remain. Their names are Joseph Gould, Clarence Gould, residing in Gouldtown, and Nancy, wife of George W. Gould, with a home in Atlantic City. Mason Mulford Gould married Elizabeth, daughter of Richard and Amelia Pierce, who lived on the road to Roadstown, owning the farm now owned by Gottleib Gosman. They had seven daughters but no son. The daughters are all living and married, excepting one, the wife of E. P. Wilson, of Pleasantville, N. J. She died several years ago. Joseph died as a young man; Moses married Elizabeth, daughter of Adrian Pierce. Both are dead. Their only son, Mitchell H. Gould, is their sole survivor; Mitchell Gould has only one daughter, the wife of Smith Gould, Jr., of Bridgeton.

Leonard Gould, the youngest son of Abijah and Hannah Pierce Gould, married Almeda, daughter of John and Tabitha Murray. They also resided on a sixty-acre patrimony of the original Gould estate, just south from the farms of his brothers Benjamin and Furman and eastward and adjoining that of his other brother, Abijah, and southeast from his brother Richard Gould. They had three sons, Jeremiah Gould, Clayton Gould and Ephraim Gould. Clayton is still living, a very old man — of ninety-one. They also had six daughters, Eliza Ann, Rachel, Emeline, Mary, Harriet, and Clara. Harriet became the second wife of Anthony Gould, 2nd, as already shown. Jeremiah married Louisa, daughter of Richard and Amelia Murray Pierce; Clayton married Harriet Pierce, daughter of Anthony and Sarah Jones Pierce; Ephraim went away and married among colored people; Eliza Ann became the second wife of Daniel Lee of Salem, and had several sons, among them being Benjamin F. Lee of Flemington, N. J.; Rachel married Jonathan Cuff, and resided on a farm in Salem County; her husband died many years ago, and she resides with one of her sons on a large farm in Salem County. She is now eighty-eight years of age. Mary married Francis Cuff, of Salem; he was a son of Archibald and Lydia Gould Cuff. They were always successful Salem County tenant farmers residing on large, well-stocked farms among Quakers. They had a numerous family, and both are now dead. Emeline married Reuben Pierce, Jr., son of Reuben Pierce and Ann Cuff Pierce — they resided in the city of Salem, and had one child, but all three are dead. Clara married Jacob Coombs, and has always resided in Gouldtown. Jacob Coombs' mother was Elizabeth, daughter of Anthony Pierce, 2nd, his father was William Coombs, a Philadelphian. Jacob and Clara Coombs had several children. Jacob died suddenly about two years ago, over eighty years of age. Clara, his widow, is living.

The youngest son of Benjamin Gould, 1st, was Elisha Gould, who, as has been already shown, married Elizabeth, youngest daughter of Richard and Hannah Van Aca Pierce. Elisha was born in 1755, and Elizabeth, who died in 1836, was a few years younger, being born about 1760. Their children were Pierce Gould, born 1785; Charlotte, 1786; Elisha, 1788; Elijah, 1790; Jesse, 1792; Elizabeth, 1794; Sarah, 1795.

Pierce Gould married Sarah Murray, widow of Menon Pierce, 2nd, who had one child, Maurice, who, when he grew up, went to Mount Holly. This Sarah was the daughter of John and Tabitha Murray. Pierce Gould and his wife, Sarah, had children, Elizabeth, Caroline, Augustus, Fanny, and Frederick. The latter is the only one alive.

Elizabeth married Charles Cato, of Salem; they had but one child, Elizabeth, still living in Bridgeton, but who never married. Caroline married Robert Pierce, son of Jesse Pierce and Christina Stoms Pierce, and they had two children; one of whom survives and is the second wife of the aged Clayton Gould. Her first husband was Isaac Wood, a white man residing on a farm on the road from Indian Fields to Rosenhayn. Fanny married Elijah Gould, 2nd, son of Richard Gould, and had two daughters, Julia and Malvena. Julia married Andrew Pierce of Salem, and Malvena married Abijah Gould, 4th, now residing in Gouldtown; he is the only survivor of the family of his father, Oliver Gould, son of Benjamin Gould, 2nd.

Mrs. Hannah Gould, Widow of Elijah Gould, and Mother of Rev. Theodore Gould. She was the Daughter of John and Tabitha Murray.

Charlotte Gould, oldest daughter of Elisha Gould, married Richard Gould, as has been already related.

Elisha Gould, 2nd, married Mary Cuff, and their descendants have already been detailed in part, but it is well to say here that the present Smith Gould, the barber in Bridgeton, who is the only son of Smith Gould, Sr., who was the only son of Elisha Gould, has one child, an only son, who might be called a complete Gould as to immediate descent. This boy, Lenhart Gould, is the son of Smith Gould and Beatrice Gould. Beatrice Gould's parents were Mitchell Gould and Ann Gould. Mitchell was the son of Moses Gould and Elizabeth Pierce, daughter of Adrian Pierce, while Ann was the daughter of Augustus Gould and Mary Elizabeth, daughter of Adam Pierce, 2nd. Mitchell was an only son, and Moses, his father, was the brother of Maria Gould, wife of Smith Gould, 1st, therefore, little Lenhart's mother and father were both Goulds; the mother and father of Smith Gould, 2nd, were both Goulds, and the parents of Beatrice, his wife, are both Goulds.

Elijah Gould married Hannah, daughter of John and Tabitha Murray; the descendants of these two were perhaps, the most distinguished of all in Gouldtown, in the times they lived. The children were Henry and Ann, twins. Henry married Elizabeth, daughter of William and Prudence Murray Cuff, of Salem. They went to Illinois in 1854. They never had any children to live, and both are dead. Ann married J. Freeman Pierce, son of Wanaca, and brother of Holmes Pierce. Both have passed away.

The other sons were John, Theodore (Rev. Theodore Gould), and Eli Gould. John and Theodore married sisters, who were also sisters to their brother Henry's wife, Elizabeth. John married Sarah, and Theodore married Caroline, both daughters of William and Prudence Murray Cuff. Eli married Mary, daughter of James and Rebecca Gould Steward.

The other daughters were Hannah (married Robert D. Stewart), Ruth (married Moses Pierce), Sarah (married Alfred Gould). All of these have left well known descendants. Of the two sons of Rev. Theodore Gould, one is a printer in Philadelphia; the other is an electrical engineer in Boston.

When Henry and John Gould were young men they built an oyster schooner, and engaged in carrying oysters from Maurice River Cove — this industry then in its infancy — to Philadelphia, also from the Chesapeake Bay to Baltimore. After the close of the oyster season, they engaged in carrying produce and peaches from Delaware and Maryland to Baltimore and Philadelphia. This was long before the War of .the Rebellion, and was, of course, hazardous in those times, had their color been suspected. John Gould after this became a carpenter, and with his cousin, Enoch Gould, whose father, Jesse, was a carpenter, they employed a gang of workmen and erected many buildings. In those days it was the custom for a carpenter to build a house from cellar to roof; they would do the mason work, laying the cellar walls and foundations, and lath and plaster the walls. All those trades were to be found in practice among the Gouldtown men in those times. Abijah Gould, 2nd, was a millwright, an occupation for which there is now but little use.

Jesse Gould, the carpenter, married first, Mary Lippincott, a Leni-Lenape Indian; they had two sons, Enoch and James, both of whom became carpenters, and one daughter, Abigail. Mary Lippincott died. Jesse's second wife was Hannah Pierce, daughter of Menon Pierce, 1st. To this union were born Emily, and Anson. Anson died young. Emily married Abijah Gould, 3rd, father of Jesse Gould, M.D., now of Philadelphia. Hannah, this wife, died, and Jesse's third wife was Hannah Pierce again — this time a daughter of Wanaca Pierce — who was killed by lightning in August, 1819.

To Jesse Gould and this third wife were born Matilda, who became the wife of Rev. James V. Pierce; Freeman, who also became a carpenter and who married Miriam, daughter of Elisha Gould, of Salem; Hezekiah, also becoming a carpenter, and afterwards a machinist, learning this trade with the Moore Brothers, who had a machine shop between what is now South Avenue and Grove Street. Hezekiah married Malinda, daughter of Amos and Jane Murray Pierce. In 1862-63, they went to Michigan, where Hezekiah became an organ manufacturer; he left two children, and died in the West. His widow still survives, residing with her daughter and son-in-law in Canada.

Mrs. Sarah Dunn Pierce, Mother of Mrs. Jacob Wright.

Hezekiah was born at the old Jesse Gould homestead, now owned by John Stout, at the tollgate in Gouldtown. He and Matilda were the youngest. At their home the well from which they drew the water was very deep, and is still. One day Hezekiah, when a boy, drew up a bucket of water with the old style of windlass: leaning over to dump the bucket, the windlass broke out of the curb, and windlass, bucket, and boy went in a bunch down to the bottom of the well. Matilda, a half-grown girl, began screaming; and Hezekiah, from the bottom of the well, hallooed up, "Till, you needn't cry; I'm a comin' up." — and sure enough, by bracing arms and legs to the sides of the well, he scrambled to the top, but little the worse for his terrific plunge. The writer of this looked down the well that night on the way home from school.

Enoch Gould married Sarah Ann, daughter of Elisha and Mary Cuff Gould, of Salem; they had an interesting family of girls and but one son, Elisha, 3rd, who graduated from Lincoln University, but shortly afterward died. Two daughters of Enoch Gould are still living; Henrietta Shords and Olivia Dickinson.

James Gould married Charlotte, daughter of Norton Gould, both have deceased, leaving no issue; Abigail married Seneca Bishop, and they had one child, Joseph, also a graduate of Lincoln University and who also deceased soon afterward, having never married. Lydia Gould, as has been detailed, married Archibald Cuff, and afterwards Rev. Furman Gould, becoming his third wife, his second being Hannah Gould Wester. Charles Gould, 1st, married "Kitty" Gould and had three sons, as before told.

Sarah Gould married Thomas Dunn, of Salem; their children were Sarah, who married Jacob Wright and has a large family; Elizabeth, who married a man named Green and left no children; Robert Dunn, who married Christina, daughter of Anthony Gould, 2nd, and left two daughters; and Ercurious, who left three sons and one daughter, one son is now a minister. After the death of Dunn, Sarah married Anthony Pierce, 3rd.

Elizabeth Gould married Samuel Gould at first, as has been stated, and becoming a widow married Daniel Siro. This woman became blind, but she was a remarkable woman. Blind as she was, she knew all the news of the neighborhood, could detect any one whom she had once met, by their step, and could tell whether it was a man, woman, or child and whether a large person or small. She was a great plyer of the knitting needles and forever busy in darning and mending wherever she lived or visited. She stayed quite a time in the family of the writer's parents, and when we were all at home she was to us a source of pleasure and amusement, joining in our pranks with as much relish as if young and not sightless, but woe to us if we carried our sports too far.

One night having been more full of fun and frolic perhaps than usual, we were sent off upstairs to bed. Our noise and laughter continued after we got upstairs, and soon "Aunt Elizabeth," as we used to call her, came to the foot of the stairs and called out "If you young'uns don't make less noise, I'll come up there and lick you like six!" That was a new word to us then and "lick you like six" was passed around among us (but out of her hearing) for many a day.

Descendants of Benjamin Gould, 2nd, of Gouldtown, New Jersey, Living at Present and Celebrating Their Annual Reunion on the Original Home Place, August 18th, 1910.

Pedigree of Benjamin Gould

1. Benjamin Gould, I, immediate descendant of John Fenwick, through his granddaughter, Elizabeth Adams.
2. Abijah Gould, I, a son.
3. Benjamin Gould, II, a grandson.

Children

1. Lydia Gould Sheppard   2. Prudence F. Gould
(Two children now living.)

Grandchildren

1. Almond, Mary
2. Cruse, Amanda B. Lee
3. Felts, Alice S.
4. Gould, Abijah
5. Gould, Jesse, M.D.
6. Gould, Margaret S.
7. Gould, Mary S.
8. Gould, Joseph Chaplain Steward
9. Gould, Josephine
10. Gould, Clarence
11. Lloyd, Elizabeth L.
12. Gould, Nancy
13. Lee, Benjamin F., Bishop
14. Pierce, Sarah S.
15. Pierce, Isabella L.
16. Sheppard, Thomas
17. Steward, William
18. Steward, Theophilus G.,
19. Steward, Stephen S.
20. White, Jane Lee
21. Webster, Charles

(Twenty-one grandchildren now living.)

Great-Grandchildren

1. Almond, William
2. Bond, Bert
3. Bond, Berne
4. Cuff, Thomson W.
5. Gary, Kate S.
6. Dixon, Mary F.
7. Drain, Florence M.
8. Durisoe, Emma J.
9. Felts, Maggie
10. Felts, Leo
11. Felts, Justin
12. Felts, Phoebe, Teacher
13. Felts, Albertina
14. Gould, Rudolph
15. Gould, Marie
16. Gould, Leander
17. Gould, Emily
18. Gould, Cleon
19. Gould, Elizabeth
20. Gould, Jesse, 2nd
21. Gould, Menon
22. Gould, Filbert
23. Gould, Lavinia
24. Gould, Percival
25. Gould, Emily
26. Gould, Ann E.
27. Gould, Jennie B.
28. Gould, Isabella
29. Gould, Roberta
30. Gould, Edna
31. Gould, Luther D.
32. Gould, Agnes, Teacher
33. Gould, Alice
34. Gould, Sydney
35. Gould, Edgar E.
36. Gould, Leslie S.
37. Gould, Nathan
38. Gould, Viola
39. Gould, Phoebe
40. Gould, Eva
41. Gould, Carlton
42. Gould, Iona
43. Gould, Edwin
44. Gould, Milford
45. Gould, Benjamin
46. Gould, Walter
47. Glass, Maud L.
48. Gould, Jonathan
49. Gould, Grace D.
50. Felts, Harriet Webster
51. Jones, Jennie
52. Jones, Sara L.
53. Lively, Lizzie M.
54. Lloyd, Frank
55. Lloyd, Henry
56. Lloyd, Leon
57. Lloyd, Arabella
58. Lee, Sarah

59. Lee, Frances A.
60. Lee, B. F., Jr.
61. Lee, Effie
62. Owens, May
63. Pierce, Ethel
64. Pierce, Cora
65. Pierce, Tamson M.
66. Pierce, Clifton
67. Pierce, Myrtle
68. Pierce, Clara
69. Pierce, Hilda
70. Pierce, Austin R.
71. Pierce, Rebecca
72. Pierce, Ella W.
73. Sheppard, Floyd
74. Sheppard, Ernest
75. Sheppard, Lydia
76. Steward, Charles G., Dentist
77. Steward, Frank R., Lawyer
78. Steward, Benjamin G., M. D.
79. Steward, T. B.
80. Steward, G. A.
81. Steward, Clara
82. Steward, Wilmon
83. Steward, Fred K.
84. Steward, Edwina
85. Steward, Esther
86. Steward, Thaddeus
87. Steward, Charlotte
88. Thoroughgood, Jane
89. Wallace, Louisa
90. Webster, Joseph
91. Webster, William
92. Webster, Louis
93. Webster, Daniel
94. Webster, Eli
95. Webster, Frank
96. Webster, Russel
97. Webster, Gertrude
98. Webster, Earl
99. Wright, Lillie
100. White, Phoebe

(One hundred great-grandchildren now living.)

Great-Great-Grandchildren

1. Almond, William, Jr.
2. Almond, Clarence
3. Almond, Thomas
4. Almond, Maud
5. Almond, Rosell
6. Coombs, Bertha
7. Coombs, Elizabeth
8. Coombs, Jacob
9. Jackson, Justin
10. Jackson, Agnes
11. Gould, Raphael
12. Gould, Constance
13. Gould, Rex
14. Gould, Madeline
15. Gould, Douglas
16. Gould, Stanley
17. Gould, Grace
18. Gould, Byrel
19. Gould, Pearl L.
20. Gould, Clayton
21. Gould, Harry
22. Gould, Eva
23. Gould, Leonard
24. Gould, Leland
25. Gould, Lester
26. Gould, Martha
27. Gould, Sarah
28. Gould, Charlotte
29. Gould, Sarah
30. Gould, Elvira
31. Gould, Raymond
32. Gould, Susan
33. Gould, Livola
34. Gould, Oscar
35. Gould, Prudence
36. Gould, Clifford
37. Gould, Inez
38. Gould, Elizabeth
39. Gould, Helen
40. Gould, Jeanette

41. Gould, Eli
42. Gould, Marie
43. Gould, Herschel
44. Gould, Lamont
45. Lively, Lavinia
46. Lively, Eliza
47. Lively, Mary
48. Lively, Walter
49. Lloyd, Frank, Jr.
50. Lloyd, Walter
51. Lloyd, Raymond
52. Lloyd, Harry
53. Lloyd, Anna
54. Miller, Leah
55. Miller, Hannah
56. Miller, Carl
57. Pierce, Florence Lloyd
58. Pierce, Cortland
59. Pierce, Ashton
60. Pierce, Lawrence
61. Pierce, Lorenzo
62. Pierce, Oliver
63. Pierce, Margaret
64. Pierce, Annabel
65. Pierce, Dora
66. Pierce, Roy K.
67. Pierce, Earl G.
68. Pierce, Romaine I. H.
69. Pierce, Jessie H.
70. Pierce, Vernon Philip
71. Pierce, Hartley Rupert
72. Pierce, Terrance Claire
73. Pierce, Irving
74. Sheppard, Thomas, Jr.
75. Steward, Stephen, Jr.
76. Steward, Raymond
77. Steward, Leon
78. Steward, Harold
79. Webster, Eva
80. Webster, Ruth
81. Webster, Oscar
82. Wright, Ethel
83. Wynder, Cora
84. Webster, Virginius
85. Cuff, Vivian
86. Cuff, Grafton
87. Cuff, Mildred
88. Cuff, Russel
89. Cuff, Gertrude
90. Felts, Mary Alice
91. Felts, Ruth
92. Felts, George W.
93. Jones, Elizabeth
94. Lee, Benjamin F., III

(Ninety-four great-great-grandchildren now living.)

To this list might be added the names of eight little great-great-grandchildren, who are living, — babies at the time of this writing, — making a total of two hundred and twenty-three from one grandson of Benjamin Gould, 1st.

Chapter Eleven - The Cuffs of Salem; Their Probable Origin; Their Ultimate Connection with the Gould, Pierce, and Murray Families

The Cuff family was of slave origin, though in a time quite remote; Cuff, a slave, was owned by a man named Padgett. Padgett had three daughters, and he, by some means, got into the Continental Army, in the French and Indian War, and was killed.

Cuff took care of the widow, and she finally married him. He was called "Cuffee Padgett"; they had three sons, and when these went to school they were taunted by the other boys as being the sons of "Old Cuffee Padgett;" so they would have their father drop the Padgett and take the name of Cuffee Cuff. The names of these sons were Mordecai, Reuben, and Seth. The grave of Cuffee Cuff is in the colored burying ground at Canton, N. J., the land for which was given by his oldest son, Mordecai, and his is the first grave in it. Mordecai dug the grave himself for his father, and while digging it, his little daughter, Dorothy, was playing about; on the fence nearby she found a gold chain hanging, which it was supposed was lost by some young people from Philadelphia who had been there the day before. She kept this chain for years and before her death gave it to her son, Jacob B. Pierce, of Gouldtown, an old man now, who still has it at this time (December, nineteen hundred and twelve).

These three brothers, sons of Cuffee Cuff, became farmers; but later, Reuben became a preacher in the Methodist Society, and organized a church in Salem, and was one of the founders of the African Methodist Episcopal Church in America. Reuben kept a Bible record of his own family. The Bible is now in possession of Wm. A. Cuff, of Bridgeton.

This record shows that he was born in Salem, March 28, 1764, and he left numerous descendants, for he had a large family. His brother, Seth, married, and had three daughters, Mary, Sarah, and Emma Ann; the two last died young. Reuben Cuff, the preacher, married Hannah Pierce, the record states. She was born November, 1767. They were married March 3, 1790. She was the daughter of Richard Pierce, 1st, of Gouldtown. Their children were Anthony, born December 18, 1790; Jonathan, June 20, 1792; Reuben, April 4, 1794, died very young; Richard, March 28, 1796; Alley, 1798, died September 11, 1799, aged one year, nine months, and twenty-one days; Anna, December 29, 1799; Elizabeth, February 21, 1802; Reuben (named after the one who died), March 7, 1804. Hannah, the wife and mother, died April 23, 1804, a little more than a month after the birth of her last son.

Reuben Cuff, the father, on November 28, 1805, took for his second wife, Lydia Iler, widow of Morris Her. To them were born Burgoyne, October 12, 1806, and Archibald, date not given, also one daughter, Caroline, who married Daniel Lee, uncle of Bishop B. F. Lee, but she died early, childless. Lydia, the second wife of Reuben, the preacher, died May 2, 1814, and two years after this he married Ann Gould, daughter of Samuel Gould of Gouldtown, May 1, 1816. In this year Rev. Reuben Cuff attended the convention in Philadelphia as a delegate, in the organization of the African Methodist Episcopal Church, as before stated.

Anthony Cuff, the oldest son, married Martha, the second daughter of Anthony Gould, 1st, of Gouldtown. She was the granddaughter of Benjamin and Ann Gould, founders of Gouldtown. Their children were Mordecai, Anthony, and William Cuff, and Phoebe Hannah, and another daughter, who died early in life. Their youngest son, William Cuff, still dwells in Bridgeton and is now (1912) in his seventy-fifth year. He has one daughter living. Phoebe Hannah married Hosea Pierce, son of Reuben Pierce, and great-grandson of Anthony and Mary Van Aca Pierce. Three daughters were born to them; she died early in her married life. Jonathan Cuff married Mary, daughter of John and Tabitha Murray of Gouldtown. Their children were Jonathan, Jr., Oliver, Margaret, Jane, Leonard, Mary, Artie, and Thomas. Richard Cuff married Rebecca Thompson. Three sons and three daughters are still living; one son, Hiram Cuff, a farmer, resides in Salem County, one daughter, Hannah, wife of Charles Cuff, resides in Salem County, another, wife of Jeremiah Harris, resides in Holly Beach, New Jersey, and the other two sons reside in East Jersey. Rebecca, the youngest, resides in Bridgeton.

Elizabeth married William Wilson, a noted Salem County farmer in his day. They had several sons and but one daughter, all of whom are now dead, except William and Joseph, both over eighty years old and residing in Philadelphia.

William Wilson, Jr., married Anna, daughter of his mother's brother, Archibald Cuff. Two sons and one daughter are also living, but Anna died many years ago. Joseph Wilson married Tamson Sheppard, daughter of Lydia Gould Sheppard (daughter of Benjamin and Phoebe Gould), the woman who recently died at the age of one hundred and two. Tamson had but one child, which died an infant, and she deceased in 1874, aged thirty-five.

Reuben Cuff married Tamson Cox, widow of William Cox, of Indian descent, if not a half-breed. There were no children born to them. She also was the daughter of Benjamin and Phoebe Gould, and died in 1877 in Gouldtown.

Burgoyne married Prudence, daughter of Benjamin Pierce, of Gouldtown. He was a well-to-do farmer near Quinton. They had but one child, Burgoyne, Jr., who became a preacher, but died early in life. He married, however, Estelle, daughter of Robert Dunn, of Gouldtown; they had no children.

Mordecai Cuff, brother of Rev. Reuben and Seth Cuff, married Margaret ("Peggy") Thomas, sister to David Murray's wife, and had three daughters, Ruhamah. Prudence and Dorothy. Ruhamah became the wife of Oliver Gould, oldest son of Benjamin and Phoebe Gould, and resided in Gouldtown. Prudence married Lewis Pierce, son of Anthony Pierce, of Gouldtown, and resided in Harmersville, where he kept a general store. After Prudence's death Dorothy became Pierce's second wife and had children. She became the second wife of Elisha Gould, Jr., of Gouldtown, and died in 1894, aged eighty-four. They had no children. Archibald Cuff, Rev. Reuben's son, married Lydia Gould, daughter of Elisha Gould, and they had sons and daughters. Their sons were Seth, still living, and now over ninety years old; Elisha, Burgoyne, Reuben, Francis, Daniel, Archibald and Charles; and daughters, Anna and Caroline. Anna, Caroline and Francis are dead, all the others survive. Archibald Cuff erected a small home on land left to his wife by her father Elisha Gould, which stood in front of where the Gouldtown church now stands. It was burned down, and the family then removed to Salem, where he engaged in farming until his death. His widow, many years after, became the second wife of her cousin. Rev. Furman Gould.

The Bible record has become so dulled by age that some of the dates are undecipherable. A son, William, one of the older children, but not the oldest, has his record entirely obliterated. He married Prudence Murray, daughter of John and Tabitha Murray, of Gouldtown, and became a tenant farmer in Salem County, residing on the same rich farm until he had raised a large family, when he died, and his son Job succeeded him on the same farm until he also raised a large family, and now lives retired in Hancock's Bridge.

Five of William and Prudence Cuff's daughters became the wives of Goulds: one, Hannah Ann, was married by Jonathan Gould, residing in Gouldtown; Elizabeth, another, married Henry Gould, and removed to Illinois, where she died; another, Hester, married Furman Gould, Jr., and resided in Bridgeton; another, Sarah J., married John Gould, the well-known carpenter and builder in his day, and another, Caroline, is the wife of Rev. Theodore Gould, of Philadelphia. They had four sons, William, Jr., Joseph, Job, and David. William married Maranda Murray, daughter of his mother's brother, Oliver Murray, of Gouldtown; Job married Lydia Ann, daughter of Aaron Gould, of Gouldtown; Joseph never married and died an old bachelor several years ago, and David went away some thirty years ago or more, and lost his identity.

Elisha Gould, Jr., married Mary, daughter of Seth Cuff; they had one son. Smith, who married Maria, daughter of Abijah Gould, Jr., and Rachel Hicks Gould, and four daughters, Sarah Ann, who became the wife of Enoch Gould, Miriam, who married Freeman Gould, Isabelle, who married Burgoyne Cuff, and Hannah Caroline, the wife of William H. Gould.

Thus the Cuff family became united with the Gould and Murray as well as the Pierce families of Gouldtown.

Chapter Twelve - Genealogical Sketch of John Murray's and David Murray's Families and Some of the Pierce Connections

John Murray married Tabitha Lupton (white). Their children were John Murray, 2nd, Oliver Murray, Silas Murray (deceased — leaving no issue), Hannah Murray, Sarah Murray, Almedia Murray, Mary Murray, Prudence Murray, Hester Murray, Jane Murray.

Oliver Murray married Amy Murray, daughter of David and Sarah Murray; their children were Maranda, who married William Cuff, Jr., of Salem; Adeline, who became the wife of the Rev. Jehu Pierce; Tabitha, who married Jeremiah Pierce, of Salem; Silas, 2nd, Wesley, and David Murray, Jr.; Sarah Murray, who married William Murray, son of John Murray, 2nd; Rachel Murray, who married Moses Pierce, 2nd; Cynthia Murray, who married David Pierce. Silas, Wesley, and David are dead.

John Murray, 2nd, married Mary Hand (white). Their children were John Murray, 3rd, Zachariah Murray, Ebenezer Murray, Henry Murray, Hiram Murray, William Murray, Lewis Murray, and daughters, Mary, Elizabeth, Julia, Harriet. All are gone, excepting Mary (Mrs. Frederick Gould), and Elizabeth, who is single and resides with Mary, and Henry. Lewis never married, and died in Millville, where he had resided since coming home from the Civil War, in which he and three of his brothers served. These four boys served in the Civil War, as white soldiers. Three of them, Hiram, Henry, and Ebenezer, served in Co. B, 2nd Regt., N. J. Vol. Infantry.

Hannah Murray married Elijah Gould, as detailed in preceding pages; Sarah Murray married first Menon Pierce, 2nd; had one son, Maurice, and after the death of Menon married Pierce Gould; Almeda Murray married Leonard Gould, youngest son of Abijah Gould, 1st, as has been before shown. Mary Murray married Jonathan Cuff, of Salem, already detailed. Prudence Murray married William Cuff, Sr., of Salem. This has been before given.

Hester Murray married Jacob Pierce, son of Wanaca Pierce. They had a numerous family. One of the sons was Jacob Pierce, who went West before the war; went to the war, rose to the rank of Captain in a regiment from the State in which he resided. After the war he married, and became owner of several large farms. In a letter received from him by the writer, some sixteen years ago, he stated he and his boys were in the height of their wheat harvest; the letter set forth that he was running eight wheat-headers, four horses each in his wheat-field at home, harvesting their grain. He said the price of wheat at that time was ninety cents per bushel. Of course, he and all his family were white people. He died about three years ago.

The other sons were Jehu, a Methodist minister; Israel, now deceased, leaving one child; Freeman, who married a daughter of Mason M. Gould; Ephraim, who married Mary Pierce, daughter of Moses Pierce, 1st; and Fayette, who married Anna Billingsly, of Philadelphia. The daughters of Jacob and Hester Pierce were Elvira, who married Aaron Pierce (both are dead, but left several children); Hester, who married William Coombs, Jr. (she is dead, leaving two sons); Hannah, who married Leonard Cuff, of Salem, who left several sons; Eliza Jane, wife of Horatio Pierce (dead, no children surviving); Almedia Jones — now a widow with one son; Cynthia, who married Robert Pierce, who died. She is now second wife of William Coombs, Jr.

Jane Murray, the youngest daughter, married Amos Pierce, son of Anthony Pierce, 2nd. Their children were Malinda, who married Hezekiah Gould; Gideon Pierce, the well-known boss carder in the East Lake Woolen Mills, in their palmy days; Robert Pierce, the boss spinner in the same works, and Lorenzo, twin brother of Robert, the "picker" in the same business; Ruth Pierce (Mrs. Valentine); Sarah Jane, wife of William Cuff, 3rd (she is deceased); Margaret, widow of Eh Lee, of Salem, and now the second wife of Stephen S. Steward, and Elizabeth, widow of Phineas Pierce of Salem.

John Murray and Tabitha Lupton, his wife, were born and lived between the years of 1750 and 1852, John dying at a little over one hundred and two years of age, and his wife at ninety-six. The youngest of their descendants named in these preceding pages is Elizabeth, the youngest daughter of Jane Murray — youngest daughter of John and Tabitha Murray.

There has been but little of drama in all the lives of these generations, above that of hard struggles to make a living; but as it can be traced, there was much of romance, some pathos, and plenty of humor throughout. John and Henry Gould, the oystermen, had much fun among themselves when they would arrive home from carrying peaches and grain from slaveholding territory; they would regale their friends at home with their experiences and relate to them the possible consequences should they be discovered to maintain a trace of the colored people's blood in themselves. Isaac Cox, when penetrating into the heart of Georgia, as far as Augusta during the Civil War, as an English blockade runner, found much romantic food to feast on when taken into the homes of those proud Georgians and feasted as an Englishman. Another, who had been a clerk in his father's country store, and later in a Salem city store, went to a large western city and became, and is, a leading drygoods merchant. But these bits of romance carry their terrors. This same merchant, now very old, sent his children (he had married there) to the fashionable schools. One day his children came home and in their lively prattle, related how some new scholars had come to their school and said they had come from Salem, New Jersey, where they knew people of the same name as theirs, — "But papa," said the children, "they said these people were colored people." Instantly terrified at a possible discovery, the father made immediate arrangements to have his children placed in an advanced and more select school.

This American prejudice is a terrible handicap to intelligent aspirations and effort. For people of the conditions herein attempted to be described to amount to anything of recognized worth and escape the galling effects of this trait of the American character, — to escape humiliation and even insult and injury, unfair and even brutal treatment, — they must leave this country, their home for generations and go to some Latin country to the southward or else to Europe. None can appreciate this situation, except those who have lived in it and felt its stifling atmosphere. "Where ignorance is bliss 'tis folly to be wise," is a saying that goes; these early children of the woods and forests knew but little of this ill thing in the early days. It has come with the advance of civilization; where they were in ignorance of the outside world they were not hurt by its rough edges. To chop their logs, plough their grounds, live on their own lands and dig their sustenance, meagre as it may have been, from their own forests, they lived in peace and simple happiness, undisturbed by those things which, with education and culture, civilization and accomplishments and increasing sensitiveness, become so galling and unbearable. It is only the clannish love of "the old home" which keeps such people here. To be distinguished, they must go to Paris, like H. O. Tanner, or to Berlin, like J. G. Bias, or to Rome or Naples, like others connected with these people this book aims to describe and illustrate in their humble, simple lives.

In 1802 Wanaca Pierce purchased from Abraham Sayre forty-five and a half acres of land out of the Abinadab Westcott estate, out towards the Beaver Dam, for which he paid £70. John Pierce, his brother, purchased from the David Westcott estate out of the Pamphylia Tract, fifty acres near Wanaca's tract, for which he paid £100. This was in 1802 also. Abraham Sayre also bought of Benjamin Pierce a tract of land in the same locality, which Benjamin had purchased of his brother John. Menon Pierce, another brother, purchased of Jacob Steeling, administrator of Anthony Gould, 1st, in 1803, thirty-four and one-quarter acres of land of which Anthony Gould died seized; this was contiguous to other lands which Menon Pierce owned and also adjoining lands purchased by his brothers, Wanaca, John and Benjamin. These lands went out towards the Beaver Dam, in what was long known as Lebanon Neck. Richard, their brother had purchased land just north from Gouldtown. Another brother, Anthony, 2nd, had already owned a measure of land close to the lands of Benjamin Gould, 1st.

Jonathan Freeman Pierce, Son of Wanaca and Mary Pierce.

From these six brothers descended that branch of Pierces, the progeny of Richard and Hannah Wanaca Pierce. They were born between 1750 and 1770. Richard and Anthony were in the Revolution. They intermarried mostly with the Murrays and Goulds.

Wanaca Pierce married Mary Murray, daughter of Othniel Murray. They had children, Adrian, born in 1802, Peleg, Jacob, Jesse, Wanaca, Jr., all older than Adrian, and Isaiah, J. Freeman, and Holmes, all younger than Adrian; and daughters, Hannah, Catherine, Lydia, and Mary. Wanaca and Mary — father and daughter — were killed by lightning while standing in the door of their home in August, 1819.

Adrian Pierce married Rachel Stewart, daughter of Cato and Elizabeth Stewart. Rev. Jeremiah H. Pierce was one of their sons. Stewart H. Pierce of Carmel, who resides on the old homestead of his father, is the only one of the family now living. Jacob Pierce married Hester Murray, and their descendants have been given in preceding pages. Jesse Pierce married Ruth Pierce Duck, a widow, who was his cousin, and daughter of his uncle, Benjamin Pierce. They had no children, but Ruth had two children, Amos and Prudence Duck, by her former marriage. Peleg was unmarried. Isaiah married Jane Pierce, daughter of Richard Pierce, 3rd, and had one child; Mrs. Jane Keen, residing in Bridgeton, is a granddaughter.

J. Freeman Pierce married Ann Gould, daughter of Elijah Gould, 1st; one daughter and one son are still living. Holmes Pierce married Mary Baracliff, a German woman; they left several children, prominent of whom is the enterprising farmer and wood-dealer, George T. Pierce, or Pearce as he spells his name. Holmes always spelled his name in the same way, declaring that was the original name. Holmes Pierce was an energetic and enterprising man and left quite a fortune when he died a few years ago. Hannah Pierce became the second wife of Jesse Gould, as previously related, and Catherine married Aaron Gould; Lydia married Rev. Henry Davis, and left no children; both died years ago.

Holmes Pierce.

Adrian Pierce owned about seven hundred acres of woodland and farm land — most of it woodland, but it has nearly all been sold off by his heirs. Holmes Pierce left much property in farm land and woodland, besides several houses in Bridgeton; he left each of his sons, Peter, John, Holmes, Jr., and George a farm, and his only daughter, Sophia, a portion in cash.

George, the most enterprising of the sons, has added largely to his patrimony, both in woodland and in city property. He also owns the homestead farm, where his father resided before retiring and moving into the city. George also owns his father's city home, on East Commerce Street, near which he has recently purchased the seventy-acre farm and residence owned by the late Nathan Gould, now within the city limits of Bridgeton.

Wanaca Pierce, 1st, left considerable property, mostly timberland, which was divided by his administrators among his children. Jacob Pierce, J. Freeman Pierce, Wanaca Pierce, Jr., as well as Adrian and Holmes, all added considerably to their original patrimonies, but the others did not. Wanaca Pierce,

Jr., purchased a farm eastward from Fairton, where he lived and died, and after his death the farm was purchased by John Gould.

Holmes Pierce was the youngest son, and seemed to have inherited the shrewd instinct of his father for progressiveness, more than the others, judging by the traits of his father's character as handed down. Holmes early started out to make money, as his father's death occurred when he was quite young. Having a fair education he taught school for a short time, and then he became a medicine peddler, but this was too slow to suit his notion of making money, and he went into buying and selling cattle; purchasing a farm, he went into horse-breeding. Soon he became one of the heaviest dealers in the county in cord-wood, hoop-poles and salt hay. No man around the county employed more men in these enterprises than did Holmes Pierce. Next to him in the cordwood and hoop-pole business in those contemporary times, however, were Oliver and Abijah Gould, 3rd, who engaged many men and teams in these industries a half century ago and more. The salt hay which Holmes Pierce dealt in was mostly used for packing hay in the glass-works in South Jersey and in Philadelphia and in the pottery works at Trenton, where hundreds of tons were sold annually.

Sketches of the David and Sarah Murray Family

The children of David and Sarah Thomas Murray were Othniel, 2nd, Jeremy, Amy, Sarah, Patience, Charity, Hope (the last three were triplets), Elizabeth, Amelia, Nancy, Enos, Mary, Margaret.

Othniel Murray, 2nd, married Angeline Pierce, daughter of Richard Pierce, 2nd, and Tabitha Pierce, daughter of Adam Pierce, 1st, the Revolutionary soldier. Othniel and Angeline had several children; one daughter and one son are still living, and one of the son's sons, Othniel, 3rd, is now in the United States Army, stationed at Fort Reno, at this writing. The daughter and son who survive, reside in Bridgeton.

Jeremy lived a bachelor until quite an old man, when he married a widow, who came from Tennessee; both are long dead, leaving no children. Amy Murray married her cousin, Oliver Murray, and had a number of children, who have been heretofore enumerated. Sarah Murray married Charles Lloyd, a manumitted black slave, who used to drive a team in the great gangs of freight wagons which conveyed merchandise from Baltimore to Pittsburgh, before the days of railroads. Their children were William, Adelia, Sabia, George, Charles, Lydia, Emily, Amanda, Alexander, Jonathan, Lewis, and Albert. Of these Charles, George, Jonathan, and Albert of the boys, and perhaps Lydia, Emily, and Amanda, are still living.

Patience Murray married Clement Pierce, stepson of Wanaca Pierce, 1st. They had many children; all are dead or gone away. Charity married a man named David Baily, and resided in Salem County. They had two children, David J. Baily and Nancy. Nancy became the wife of Levi Harmon, of Back Neck. Both David and Nancy are dead. Hope Murray, the last of the triplets, was drowned when a young man. Amelia married Richard Pierce, 3rd, son of Richard, 2nd, and Tabitha Pierce, and resided on a farm which they owned on the Roadstown road — now owned by Gottlieb Gosman.

Elizabeth Murray married John Keen, a white man. They were married by the venerable Ethan O shorn, pastor of the "Old Stone Church" in Fairfield, in January, 1839. Their children were John Keen, Jr., who became a shoemaker; Joseph and Levi, who went to Virginia and settled after the war, as white men, and Jacob Jones, who died in Gouldtown; Marietta, a very beautiful girl, long dead, and Margaret, wife of Aaron Paul Gould, now living; Marietta was the wife of Jacob B. Pierce — she left no children.

Nancy Murray married a colored man in Salem. Enos died young. David married a daughter of Simon and Mary Siro, but died without issue.

The children of John and Tabitha Lupton Murray have been enumerated. The children of David and Sarah Thomas Murray have also been enumerated. Mark Murray married Hannah Gates, August 23, 1810. All of these women were white. Mark resided on what was long called "The Mark Fields," which are beyond Gouldtown and a little northward from the old Dick farm on the Millville trolley-line. The Mark fields are now owned by George W. Coombs. Mark Murray ran away; what became of his wife is not known. They left no children. The children of the sister, Mary Murray, who became the wife of Wanaca Pierce, 1st, have been given with their descendants.

Dorcas Murray, the remaining sister, became the wife of Adam Pierce, the Revolutionary soldier, who was the only son of Anthony and Mary Van Aca Pierce, as has been stated.

The children of Adam and Dorcas Pierce were Matthias, Andrew, Asa, and Adam, and three daughters. Asa died young; Matthias went as a sailor in a vessel belonging to John Trenchard of the original Trenchard family, of Fairfield, and in one voyage, on which a son of Trenchard, the owner, was a sail-

Mrs. Elizabeth Stewart, One of the Organizing Members of Gouldtown Church

or, the vessel was lost with all on board and nothing was ever heard from her or any of her crew.

Andrew Pierce got in a scrape by cutting the spokes out of the wagon wheels of Benjamin Gould, 2nd; and, to avoid arrest, ran away and never came back.

Adam Pierce, the youngest son, was born in the year 1800; his wife was Juliann, daughter of Cato and Elizabeth Hicks Stewart. They had six sons and two daughters. The daughters were Mary Elizabeth, wife of Augustus Gould (both now dead); Sarah Rachel, wife of the present writer; Edward, who married Rebecca Bustill, of Philadelphia; Alexander, who went West, and died several years ago in Tiacoma, Washington, leaving a widow but no children; John C, who died in Bridgeton, leaving two sons; Calvin B. and Warren W. Pierce; Benjamin F., who resides at Fairton and whose wife is Sarah, second daughter of Lydia Gould Sheppard, who died recently in Millville at the great age of one hundred and two years. Charles Jones, the next of the brothers, died in Cedar Rapids, Iowa, leaving a widow, but no children. Hosea, the youngest child, died a youth.

Edward Pierce left three sons, one daughter, and a widow still surviving. Two sons, the daughter and the mother reside in Philadelphia, while the oldest son, Edward Pierce, Jr., resides in Washington and has been for many years in the Government employ. Benjamin F. Pierce has six daughters and one son, all living; one daughter resides in Tacoma, Washington.

The daughters of Adam and Dorcas Murray Pierce were Sarah, who married John Flemmings, of Yorktown; Violette, who married David Pierce, son of Richard Pierce, 2nd, and Louisa; and Tiabitha, who became the second wife of Richard Pierce, 2nd, the father of her sister's husband, David Pierce, and Hannah, who married Abram Winrow, of Stowe Creek.

David and Violette Pierce lived on a farm in Dutch Neck, where they reared a large family. Their sons were Adam, 3rd, Moses, Asa, Hosea, and the daughters Matilda, Hester, Caroline, and Priscilla.

Adam married Elizabeth, daughter of Abijah Gould, 2nd, and Rachel Hicks Gould, and had numerous children, many of whom are still living; Moses mai'ried Ruth, daughter of Elijah Gould, 1st, and Hannah Murray Gould: Moses lived on a farm he owned out near where Rosenhayn is now located; he had several daughters and two sons, most of whom are yet alive; Asa Pierce died, leaving no issue; Hosea married Sarah, daughter of Robert Anderson: Hosea was a soldier of the Civil War — he and his wife are both dead, but numerous children and grandchildren survive them; Matilda became the wife of Norton Gould, son of Richard and Charlotte Gould, and many of their children still survive; Hester Pierce became the wife of Smith Pierce, of Salem; she had one daughter and two sons, still living; Caroline Pierce married a man in Bushtown and vanished from her relations; Priscilla never married and died an old maid. David and Violette Pierce were married, July 12, 1811, the ceremony being performed by Squire James Clark of Fairfield; in the same year David's father, Richard Pierce, married his second wife, Tabitha, who was Violette's sister. This marriage ceremony was performed by the venerable Ethan Osborn, of the Old Stone Church.

Wanaca Pierce's (2nd) family

Wanaca Pierce, 2nd, married Margaret, daughter of Richard and Tabitha Pierce. He resided on the farm he bought eastward from Fairton; he had sons, Wanaca, 3rd, Cornelius, Richard, 3rd, and one daughter, Mary. They are all dead.

Wanaca's wife, Margaret, died and he again married; this time an English woman, Fanny Horton; they had two daughters (one of whom is dead), and one son now living.

The Benjamin Pierce (3rd) family

Benjamin Pierce's (3rd) wife was Margaret Murray. They had a numerous progeny; their sons were Elam, John, Henry, Benjamin, Jr., Leonard, and Charles; and daughters Margaret, Mary, and Ruth.

Ruth and Mary died unmarried; Margaret married Stratton Hicks, son of. Andrew and Sarah Pierce Hicks (one son, Andrew, lives); Elam Pierce, growing up into a fine large man, over six feet tall, went away and was lost to his family; John Pierce married a daughter of Clement Pierce, and resided in the vicinity of Seeley's Mill; they had several children, most of whom have left this part of the country; Henry married and resided in Elmer; his children are in Camden, Philadelphia, and Salem County; Leonard and Charles, the remaining sons, died unmarried.

Miscellaneous Branches of Pierce Families

The Pierce families scattered about Salem County are the descendants, mostly, of Anthony and Marie (Mary) Pierce. They are spread about Salem City, Canton, and Quinton; also formerly in Penton and latterly in Seeley and Elmer, New Jersey. Those who descended from Anthony, through Anthony, 2nd, were those about Canton, the descendants of F. Lewis and Reuben Pierce, sons of Anthony, 2nd.

Reuben had three sons, Reuben, 2nd, Smith, Thomas, and one daughter, Elizabeth. Reuben, 2nd, married Emeline, daughter of Leonard Gould, of Gouldtown; they had but one daughter, Emeline: they resided in the city of Salem, where they had a pretty home. Both Emeline and her daughter were of remarkable beauty, and Reuben, the husband and father, was a handsome man, both in form and features; his appearance was that of a Spaniard. They were a devoted family to one another, and their happy home was the subject of comment among their friends a half-century or more ago. Death, it is said, loves a shining mark, and all these died young; and in the sixties the entire family was obliterated, leaving no descendants.

Smith Pierce married Mary Cuff and left several children, Jeremiah, a Salem carpenter being the principal one now living. Thomas Pierce, the other son of Reuben, Sr., married in Camden; but they left several children surviving, some of whom lately removed to Bridgeton where they, now reside. Elizabeth married a man named Bond, in Camden, where she still resides, though advanced in years. She was a beautiful girl when young. Her husband is dead.

The children of John Pierce, at least some of them, settled in Salem, about Canton and Quinton. From these came George Pierce, who married Julia Noble, and Andrew Pierce, who married Lydia Cornish. Anthony Pierce, 3rd, son of Menon Pierce of Gouldtown, also went early into Salem County, where he married and had several children, one of whom is Menon, 4th, and from this branch came William H. Pierce, the well-known express carter of Bridgeton.

Benjamin Pierce's wife's name was Ruth (last name unknown), a German woman. She was of a very lovable character; devoted to her family and generally beloved by the neighborhood in which she lived, and familiarly called "Aunt Ruth." Their children were Benjamin, Jr., Andrew, Ruth, and Sarah. Benjamin, 2nd, married Margaret, daughter of David Murray. Ruth married Charles Duck, and Sarah married Andrew Hicks, son of Josiah and Elizabeth Pierce Hicks.

The children of Sarah Pierce and Andrew Hicks were Catherine, who married Hiram Pierce, and this family is now extinct; Rachel, who married a colored man of Salem; Sarah Ann, who went blind; Stratton, who married his cousin, Margaret, daughter of his Uncle Benjamin Pierce, his mother's brother; and Isaiah, who became a city barber in Philadelphia, and if he ever married it is not known, as he died a young man.

The youngest of the children of Andrew and Sarah Hicks was Prudence, who became the wife of William Hendrickson. Both of them are dead, leaving only an adopted daughter, to whom they left their little home on South East Avenue, Bridgeton, N. J. Andrew Hicks of Bridgeton is the sole survivor of the family of Andrew and Sarah Hicks. The family of Ruth Pierce Duck is extinct.

The families of John Pierce (who married a daughter of Clement and Patience Pierce) resided about Seeley, and have drifted away; Henry resided in Salem County; his descendants are all white.

There is another branch of the Jesse Pierce and Christina Stoms Pierce family not yet mentioned. That is the family of their son, William Pierce. Jesse and Christina Pierce had three sons and two daughters; the daughters were Almeda (wife of Anthony Gould, 2nd) and Mary, who left the neighborhood and vanished from the community; the sons were William, Ephraim, and Robert. The descendants of Robert were mentioned. James R. Pierce, of Burlington Avenue, and Ephraim Pierce, Jr., of East Commerce Street, are sons of Ephraim and Louisa Pierce. Thus two sons and two daughters of Jesse and Christina Pierce are accounted for. William Pierce, the remaining son, married Charlotte Ogden, of Hopewell Township. They had numerous children but there are only one son and three daughters of that family now living: the son Jesse, 2nd, lives alone in a small house of his own, while of the daughters, one, Elizabeth, the widow of John Murray, 3rd, resides with her daughter in Fairton. Another, Roseann, lives at Bayside, the wife of Emanuel Pierce; and Mary, the last remaining daughter, is domiciled in Greenwich. She is the widow of the late Jedediah Pierce, and has one son, Isaac Pierce, and one daughter. Rosette, now widow of Clayton Gould, 2nd, and residing in Greenwich.

Chapter Thirteen - Family Eugenics and Longevity; the Gould, Pierce, and Murray Estates

The hygienism of the Goulds, Pierces, and Murrays was of the most simple kind, and, it may be said, the most effective for the preservation of their health and the promotion of longevity; as has before been stated, all three of the families were noted for their natural length of life. Families of six to ten children would live to reach mature years, and, in many cases, all would live to reach old age. Hereditary disease was unknown among them, except as will be stated further on, unless it may be here and there in sporadic character, and not in direct heredity.

All the common infantile and youthful ailments were prevalent, such as measles, whooping-cough, chickenpox, and such like, which were almost always treated with such domestic remedies as herb teas, called "yarb tea," and poultices — according to the nature of the ailment. So far as can be ascertained, no case of smallpox or other virulent disease was ever known in the community. They took no sanitary precautions; their main treatment was to keep cool in summer and warm in winter, with plenty of solid and wholesome food, but little or no luxuries or high living. The woods afforded them the chief ingredients of their home-made medicines and salves and ointments, which were used, internally or externally, for all manner of complaints with which, in their simple lives, they were attacked.

Pulmonary troubles, except as will be explained later, were unknown; bad colds were treated with "yarb tea," fevers were dosed with home-made "yarb" febrifuge; measles were helped by infusions, and the patient kept out of a draft; for whooping-cough emetics and syrups of molasses and onions were given. Consumption, now and always such a dreadful disease, was only known sporadically, until intermarriage with one branch of the Cuff family. Its heredity seems to be positively traced in this branch, but its origin seems to be obscure.

The Goulds, Pierces, and Murrays intermarried into the Rev. Reuben Cuff family, and also the families of his brothers, Mordecai and Seth Cuff — these two last had married white women. No tuberculosis has been traced to the Rev. Reuben Cuff family directly, except in one instance, but from the families of Mordecai and Seth the trace is apparently well marked, and the inference leads to the opinion that, if hereditary, it must be by way of their marriage. Oliver Gould married a daughter of Mordecai Cuff, and had a large family of children; all but one grew to maturity and all but one died with consumption. One is still living. Elisha Gould, 2nd, married a daughter of Seth Cuff. Consumption afflicted his children and carried off many of his grandchildren, especially the family of Enoch Gould, who married Sarah Ann, the oldest daughter of Elisha Gould, 2nd. Some sporadic cases, with two or three deaths, came through the family of Anthony Cuff, whose wife was Martha Gould.

The Gould Estates

The original Gould estate, as given documentarily in the will of Benjamin Gould, 1st, was devised to his three sons, Samuel, Abijah, and Elisha. The oldest son, Anthony, was devised his portion in cash. To Samuel and Abijah, the founder gave one hundred and thirty-six acres of land to be divided equally between them, and to his remaining son, Elisha, he gave the residue of his land. The surrogate's office does not show any division of the lands left by Samuel Gould, though he left considerable. Abijah and Elisha added to their patrimony by purchase.

The estate of Elisha Gould was divided among his ten children, by order of the Orphans' Court in 1808, by three commissioners, Jedediah Davis, Jonathan Coney, and Enoch Burgen. The sons and daughters were Charles Gould, Pierce Gould, Jesse Gould, Elijah Gould, Elisha Gould, Jr., Charlotte Gould, Elizabeth Gould, Sarah Gould, Lydia Gould, and Anna Gould; the last being a minor, and dying before coming into her patrimony. The estate was divided into sixteen lots or parcels by the commissioners, and the total aggregated two hundred and one and a half acres. The report was approved by the Court August 15, 1808.

The estate of Abijah Gould, 1st, had been considerably increased before his death. His estate was also divided in 1808 by order of the Cumberland County Orphans' Court, by these commissioners: James Clark, James Westcott, and David Clark. It was divided into twenty-three lots. No. 1 to No. 23 inclusive. Hannah, the only daughter of Abijah, was given Lot No. 1 of fifty acres and sixty-seven hundredths of an acre. She died young. The report of these commissioners was approved by the court October 12, 1808. The five sons were Benjamin Gould, 2nd, Richard Gould, Abijah Gould, 2nd, Furman Gould, and Leonard Gould. In this estate was also a considerable quantity of salt marsh about Dixon's Island in Back Neck, fifty-six acres in all, and eight and a half acres of cedar swamp in Manumusken swamp, in Millville Township. The real estate of Abijah Gould, which was divided among his five sons and one daughter, was three hundred and eighty-nine and forty-seven hundredths acres, besides the salt marsh and cedar swamp.

The lands of Samuel Gould, second son of Benjamin the founder, equalled those of Abijah, 1st. This estate went to his son, Samuel, Jr.'s, widow Elizabeth, afterward Elizabeth Siro, and his daughters. Most of it is now owned by Mrs. Joseph Stewart, a large tract.

While the two estates of Abijah and Elisha Gould were thus divided among their heirs over one hundred and four years ago, the main bodies of those lands still remain in the possession of the descendants. Upon the land set off to Pierce Gould is the "God's Acre" where repose the bones of his grandparents, his parents, and himself — the ancient family burying ground. The deed for this burying ground was later, in 1827 — January 23rd — made by Pierce Gould and Sarah, his wife, to Adrian Pierce, Jesse Gould, and Benjamin Gould, trustees, and their successors forever, for the sum of one dollar, for a burying ground. Also out of this same estate, and out of that part set off to Lydia Gould, was sold one acre, deeded to Anthony Pierce, Furman Gould, Reuben Pierce, Elijah Gould, and Daniel Siro, trustees, and their successors forever for the sum of four dollars for a schoolhouse, and it is still used by the Fairfield Board of Education for that purpose. Out of the portion set off to Sarah Gould, the Trinity A. M. E. Church, in 1860, purchased a half acre, upon which the church was built and where it now stands, the deed being made to certain trustees and their successors, according to the form prescribed in the Book of Discipline of that church. The trustees at the time of the purchase and erection of the church were James Steward, Abijah Gould, Anthony Gould, Enoch Gould, and Holmes Pierce, and the minister in charge was the Rev. Joseph Smith, a man of great piety and peculiarly able administrative ability. The New Jersey Conference of the A. M. E. Church was not yet organized and this charge was still under the jurisdiction of the Philadelphia Conference, as a circuit, as it had been since the organization of the denomination in 1816, up to this time, 1860, when it became a station.

Gouldtown Graveyard

The estate of Elisha Gould, 1st, was divided by the commissioners among these ten children, all of whom were adults except Anna, who was under the age of twenty-one years, as follows: To Charles Gould, 30 acres; to Pierce

Gould, 29 acres; to Jesse Gould, 23.55 acres; to Elijah Gould, 30 acres; to Elisha Gould, 2nd, 31.25 acres; to Charlotte Gould, 13.50 acres; to Elizabeth Gould, 12.75 acres; to Sarah Gould, 11.25 acres; to Lydia Gould, 10.50 acres; to Anna Gould, 10 acres, total, 201.80 acres. These divisions are recorded in Book "D" Division of Lands, pages 322 to 331 inclusive, in the Cumberland County Surrogate's Office.

The estate of Abijah Gould, 1st, was divided into twenty-three lots, or parcels, and aggregated in acres as follows: Among his five sons and one daughter — to Benjamin Gould, 51.43 acres; to Richard Gould, 65.63 acres; to Abijah Gould, 2nd, 79.65 acres; to Furman Gould, 62.73 acres; to Leonard Gould, 79.60 acres; to Hannah Gould, 50.67 acres; total 389.71 acres. This estate had also 57-50 acres of salt marsh, and this was divided among the sons as follows: To Benjamin nine and a half acres; to Richard seventeen acres; to Abijah, Jr., twenty-three and a half acres; to Furman four and a half acres; to Leonard three acres; there was also a tract of eight and a half acres of cedar swamp in Manumuskin swamp, below Millville, and one and seventy hundredths acres of this went to each of the sons. As all this estate was left unencumbered to his children, it is evident that Abijah Gould, 1st, was a pretty thrifty man.

From this it is shown that those two ancient Goulds left to their sons and daughters almost six hundred acres of land. Anthony Gould's, 1st, land was but a small tract and was sold by his administrator, Jonathan Bowen. Samuel Gould's estate was of not much value, and was mainly bush-land of about one hundred acres, making in all seven hundred acres.

While most of these lands are still in the possession of the descendants, much has been added to them. Likewise as to old estates of the Murrays and Pierces, especially the latter, it is not far wide of the mark to say that the people of color of what is commonly known as Gouldtown, possess in the neighborhood of five thousand acres of land, the accumulations of themselves and their ancestors.

The possessions of the original Goulds were to the southward and westward of those of the original Pierces and Murrays, and this led to the northern portion being designated "Piercetown" (now called Fordsville).

Contiguous to the land of the eastern portion of Benjamin Gould the Founder's plantation, Richard and Anthony Pierce, the two brothers, had acquired a considerable number of acres. Anthony Pierce, 2nd, and Wanaca Pierce, 1st, sons of Richard, had over two hundred and twenty-five acres of farm-land and timberland between them; the southern line of Anthony's land bounded on the northern line of that part of the Gould land falling to Abijah Gould, 1st. Anthony's holding in this tract was over one hundred acres.

To the northward of this tract was a considerable scope owned by the original Murrays, while to the north and west of this was one hundred and twenty-two acres owned by Wanaca Pierce, 1st. This was originally a beautiful plot of farm- and timber-land, nearly square in shape; that is, it was a little more than one hundred and seventy-four perches long by one hundred and twelve perches in width. This is the Wanaca Pierce who, with his young daughter Mary, was killed by lightning in 1819. This man left a widow and nine other children; the oldest at that time, Wanaca, 2nd, being but twenty years old. Their mother lived many years after this, in the old homestead.

The estate of Wanaca Pierce, 1st, was divided in 1832, by commissioners appointed by the Orphans' Court as follows: To Wanaca Pierce, 2nd, nine and a half acres; to Adrian Pierce, nine acres; to Peleg Pierce, five and three-quarter acres; to Freeman Pierce, sixteen acres; to Jesse Pierce, six acres; to Jacob Pierce, fourteen acres; to Isaiah Pierce, eleven acres; to Holmes Pierce, fifteen acres; to Hannah Pierce (wife of Jesse Gould) eleven and a quarter acres; to Catherine Pierce (wife of Aaron Gould) thirteen and a half acres; to Lydia Pierce (wife of Rev. Henry Davis) twelve and a half acres; aggregating one hundred and twenty-two acres.

Between this and Anthony's land was the estate of John Murray and his brother, David Murray, while to the eastward was that of Mark Murray; these lands were of considerable extent.

Westward from the Wanaca Pierce estate, extending a mile or more, was the estate of Richard Pierce, 1st, and his other sons, Richard and John and Benjamin, while another son, Menon, owned a considerable tract further northward leaving at his death a hundred acres or more of farm and woodland out near Lebanon Neck.

Nearly all of these lands, together with additions, are still owned by the descendants of those Colonial pioneers.

Chapter Fourteen - Organization of the Church; Early Religious Affiliations of the People

Like most others of this section of New Jersey, the inhabitants of Gouldtown held to the Calvinistic doctrines, with a leaning towards Presbyterianism. Indeed, their early religious training was received from the Presbyterians. It is not unlikely that the first Benjamin Gould listened to the religious admonitions of Rev. Daniel Elmer, who came from Connecticut and was installed pastor of the church at New England town (now known as Old Stone Church) in 1729. The records of this old church were lost by a fire which destroyed the church. The earliest Goulds, as well as the Pierces and Murrays, attended this church under the administrations of Rev. Daniel Elmer; he died in 1755, the same year that Elisha, the youngest son of Benjamin Gould, the Founder, was born. They attended this church also under the administrations of Rev. William Ramsey, who was pastor of this church from 1756 and served as pastor until his death in 1771.

The Elmers always took a deep and cordial interest in Gouldtown; the descendants of Rev. Daniel Elmer being familiarly known to the people of

Gouldtown until the present time; the last Daniel Elmer, who died a few years ago (the seventh oldest son in the line of lineal descent), the son of the late Charles E. Elmer, Esq., no less so than those who had preceded him. Dr. Jonathan Elmer, a son of Rev. Daniel Elmer, born in 1745, and also his brother General Ebenezer Elmer, also a physician, practised among the early residents of Gouldtown, as did also later, Dr. Rush Bateman of Cedarville. These physicians were all Presbyterians, adherents of the New England town church, and they, especially the Elmers, did not fail to sow the seeds of their faith among the rustic people among whom they practised; Dr. (General) Ebenezer Elmer, with his son, spending many a Sunday afternoon in the first little schoolhouse in Gouldtown, catechizing the children. This is the first actual known religious teaching given in the community. The son became the distinguished Supreme Court Justice — Lucius Q. C. Elmer. The solid character of this father and son, as well as of those of their descendants, — Dr. William Elmer, Dr. Henry Elmer, Dr. Robert Elmer, John T. Nixon, later U. S. Judge (a son-in-law of Judge Elmer, always familiar with the rural community), made its impress upon these people to a lasting degree.

Rev. Ethan Osborn. Died May 1, 1858, in his 100th year. Pastor Presbyterian Church. Fairfield, 55 years.

When Rev. Ethan Osborn became pastor of the church in 1788, he gave the same care to this community that he did to others; he performed their marriage ceremonies and attended the burial of their dead. Although a Presbyterian church was organized in "Bridgetown" in 1792, the people of Gouldtown did not transfer their attendance from Fairfield.

Rev. Michael Swing, the pioneer of the Methodists in Fairfield, beginning with his advent into the community in 1799, made some impression upon the Goulds and Pierces. He built what was known as "Swing's Meeting House" in Herring Row, about 1819, for a long time the only Methodist meeting house in Fairfield. He united in marriage several Gouldtown people and held service at their funerals, but the relations of the Goulds with the Methodists were not cordial.

Miss Prudence F. Gould

The centenary of a church — any church — is always a notable event, and the Trinity A. M. E. Church at Gouldtown will, in a few more years, celebrate such an anniversary.

The Rev. Reuben Cuff, of Salem, who had become a Methodist minister, under the ministrations of Dr. Benjamin Fisler, who travelled the Salem circuit, which then extended from Salem to Cape May, married into the Gould family — Shaving wed Anna Gould — was, of course, a frequent visitor in Gouldtown, where he often held meetings in the early part of the last century. Phoebe Bowen, the wife of Benjamin Gould, 2nd, was reared in his family. Many of these meetings were held in the barn of Benjamin Gould, 2nd, on the old Gould homestead. The barn was then larger than it is now, for it has been reduced in size within the writer's recollection; it had a large threshing floor where the flail was used in the winter time, or the grain would be trodden out by the horses (which I have seen done).

This Benjamin Gould was much of a wag — though later becoming a class leader — but at these meetings he was not converted. His brother, Furman, afterward a local preacher, was with others converted. On one occasion the minister and the religious ones of the meeting tried earnest persuasion upon Benjamin (my grandfather) to induce him to join the meeting (it was not called church in those days). With much earnestness and vehemence they persuaded, bringing to bear all their arguments about everlasting damnation; making it exceedingly warm for Benjamin with their beseechings. They, at last, told him of the hot place awaiting all sinners! Slowly shaking his head he candidly replied, "I have found that out by present experience."

Benjamin later professed religion and joined the meeting. At one time, in prayer-meeting, he was called on to pray. He coolly called back, "Call on Furm, he can pray." It was long asserted that his reply was "Call on Furm, he can pray like the De'il," but this has always been denied. Let this be as it may, Benjamin Gould lived after joining the meeting a consistent, upright life, walking in the paths of piety, dying in 1851, as he had lived, a humble Christian.

The church in Gouldtown was brought together between 1816, when the denomination was formed in Philadelphia, and 1820. It was organized in Benjamin Gould's barn, but in 1823, the Westcott schoolhouse was purchased and moved into the neighborhood for the schoolhouse, where the meetings were afterwards held until the present church was built in 1860.

Miss Prudence F. Gould, the youngest daughter of Benjamin and Phoebe Gould, from papers in her possession left by her father, gives this very clear history of the church at Gouldtown, with incidents of local interest, together with a complete list of the preachers who have served as pastors from its beginning. She writes:

The records show that the first church was the old schoolhouse which stood on the old road from Fairton to Millville, on a lot near to where Lorenzo Gould now resides. This school was used also as a meeting house by the Presbyterians and

Methodists alternately, by the Westcotts, Bennetts, Seeleys, Woodruffs, and Hands (white), and by the Goulds, Pierces, and Murrays (colored). It was where most of the community attended meeting in the early part of the century (19th).

Rev. Reuben Cuff, who had organized The Methodist Society in Salem before this time, and whose first wife was a Hannah Pierce, of Gouldtown, was a frequent visitor here.

My mother, Phoebe Bowen, had been brought up in his family in Salem from a child of four years old, — her mother, Lydia Bowen, having died when she was a baby, and her father Levi Bowen, passing away when she was at the age of four, — and Rev, Reuben was a welcome visitor at our house.

After the organization of the African Methodist Episcopal Church in Philadelphia, our people thought to become attached to this denomination. By this time a series of meetings had been held at private houses, and a religious revival had sprung up. Rev. Reuben Cuff suggested the organizing of a society here. This was in 1818, and Elder Jeremiah Miller was then on the newly appointed Salem circuit, so Pastor Cuff, with the assistance of Rev. Mr. Miller, organized our society. The formal meeting was held in the home of Elizabeth Gould, widow of Elisha Gould; her house stood just north of the graveyard on the lot now owned by Albert Lloyd. The first class was organized with these fourteen members, namely: Benjamin Pierce, Furman Gould, Christiana Gould, Benjamin Gould, Phoebe Gould, Anthony Pierce, Sarah Pierce, Charlotte Gould, Elizabeth Gould, David Murray, Sarah Murray, Wanaca Pierce, Mary Pierce, and Elizabeth Stewart. Benjamin Pierce was appointed the first class leader. The society was attached to the Salem circuit and Elder Jeremiah Miller was the first preacher in charge of this appointment.

The houses being too small to accommodate the attendance, meetings were held in my father's barn, and the first Quarterly Meeting was held in June, 1819, also in my father's barn. It was a great meeting, lasting two days, and people crowded not only the bam floor, but climbed up in the mows.

The school building called the Westcott schoolhouse, which had been formerly used, and purchased by the society in 1823 and moved to the present schoolhouse lot, served the purpose of school and meeting house until the purchase of the Lummis schoolhouse in 1834. The first (Westcott) schoolhouse was sold to David Murray, who converted it into a dwelling.

The Lummis schoolhouse was moved to the site; the removal of this building was an event in the neighborhood, — several days were required to move it, and the women cooked dinners and took the meals to the men on the road. This schoolhouse was dedicated as a church by Rev. Peter D. W. Schureman, and the name given it was Ebenezer. It was so used as church and school, until the erection of the present Trinity A. M. E. Church, on the opposite side of the road — the Bridgeton and Millville turnpike.

Under the second pastorate of Rev. Jeremiah Beulah, in 1841 a split in the church occurred, resulting in the withdrawal of a number of the members who established a Methodist Episcopal Church in Fordsville. When the conference sent Rev. Mr. Beulah to the appointment for the second time, a portion of the church were bitterly opposed to him, and barred the door against him. Quite a mob was assembled to keep the preacher out of the church, Benjamin Gould and

David Murray took the preacher up on their shoulders, and while others pressed back the crowd, carried him bodily into the church. Once in the church, the opponents could not get him out. A lawsuit was entered into by his opponents to oust him; but, as the trustees of the church were in his favor, nothing came of it, and the opponents were thrown out of court.

These people, headed by Jacob Pierce and Freeman Pierce and their families and followers (excepting Freeman's wife), left the church in a body and in 1841 a schoolhouse and meeting house combined was built in Fordsville, where now they have a respectable church and a stationed pastor, and though of different denominations, the Gouldtown church and Fordsville church hold cordial and harmonious relations.

The pastors who have been in charge of the Gouldtown church from its organization are as follows:

1818. Rev. Jeremiah Miller.
1820. Rev. William Paul Quinn (afterwards Bishop).
1821. Rev. Jeremiah Ridley.
1822. Revs. J. P. B. Eddy and I. B. Dorsey (two circuit riders).
1823-25-26. Rev. Joseph Harper.
1826-28. Rev. Richard Williams.
1829. Revs. J. A. Shorts and Viley Reynolds.
1830. Revs. William Richardson, John Cornish, and Israel Scott.
1831. Revs. L. Cook and Samuel Enty.
1832. Rev. John Boggs.
1833. Rev. John Cornish.
1834-35. Rev. Peter D. W. Schureman.
1836. Revs. Noah C. W. Cannon and Henry Turner.
1837. Revs. William Moore and Levin Tilgman.
1838. Rev. Jeremiah Beulah.
1839. Rev. John Cornish.
1840. Revs. Clayton Durham and Henry C. Turner.
1841. Rev. Jeremiah Beulah.
1842-44. Rev. George Greenly.
1845. Rev. John L. Armstrong.
1846. Revs. A. W. Waymen (afterwards Bishop Waymen) and A. C. Crippin.
1847. Revs. J. R. V. Morgan, and I. B. Parker.
1848-50. Rev. Richard Barney.
1851. Rev. I. B. Parker.

1852-53. Rev. Sheppard Holcomb.
1854. Revs. Peter Gardner and Isaac Stamford.
1855. Rev. Caleb Woodyard.
1856. Revs. Henry Davis and L. Jackson.
1857-58. Rev. E. J. Hawkins.
1859. Rev. Andrew Till.
1860-61. Rev. Joseph H. Smith. At this time new Trinity Church built, at a cost of $1,600.
1862. Rev. J. H. Henson.
1863-65. Rev. Joshua Woodlin.
1866. Rev. William Watson.
1867. Rev. Joseph Nelson.
1868-70. Rev. Benjamin Darks.
1871. Rev, Leonard Patterson.
1872-75. Rev. Jos. H. Smith (second time).
1876. Rev. Redmon Faucett.
1877. Rev. Samuel B. Williams.
1878-79. Rev. E. Hammitt.
1879-80. Rev. T. C. Chambers.
1882. Rev. Geo. A. Mills.
1883. Rev. Israel Derrick.
1884-85. Rev. Alfred Garrison (who died, and Rev. James V. Pierce filled out his term).
1886-87. Rev. Wilson Peterson.
1888. Rev. H. P. Thomas.
1889-91. Rev. M. M. Dent.
1892. Rev. G. A. Mills.
1893. Rev. E. M. Harper.

1893. Rev. Geo. A. Woodson (now Dean of Payne Theological Seminary, at Wilberforce, Ohio).
1895-96. Rev. H. H. Pinkney.
1897-98. Rev. J. H. Mowbray.
1899. Rev. A. B. Cooper.
1900-03. Rev. Jas. A. Groves.
1904-05. Rev. Wm. W. Johnson.
1906. Rev. L. A. Generette.
1907-08. Rev. Aaron A. Collins.
1909-10. Rev. Geo. T. Watkins.
1911. Rev. W. W. Middleton.
1912. Rev. J. H. Robinson.

During the years 1851-52, under the pastorate of Rev. Sheppard Holcomb, a wonderful revival of religion occurred, which was most marked among the heads of families; it swept the whole community, in a measure, and a large acquisition was made to the church. A few years later, during the ministry of Rev. Jos. H. Smith, in 1860, there was another awakening, when the church membership was increased by over a score. The greatest revival in the history of the church, however, was during the winter of 1912—13 under Rev. J. H. Robinson, when in three weeks 116 were united with the church, the greatest part of whom came out of the Sunday-school.

Gouldtown A. M. E. Church

The Sunday-School

From the earliest times of its history, Gouldtown has had a Sunday-school. Even before the days when General Ebenezer Elmer and his son catechized the children, in the little old Westcott schoolhouse, Sunday instruction was given the young children of the neighborhoods in the same schoolhouse. It was not long after the regular organization of the church when a Sunday-school was kept up in the school and meeting house. This was not altogether for religious instruction exclusively, but the children were taught to spell and read and were catechized.

Jesse Gould, a cousin of Benjamin Gould, 2nd, is believed to have been the first regularly appointed Sunday-school superintendent, which position he held several years. After him was his son, Enoch Gould, who filled the position for a number of years very ably and acceptably. The best loved and most devoted Sunday-school superintendent of nearly a half century ago was Jonathan Gould, son of the preacher Rev. Furman Gould. To him the children looked up as to a kind and gentle father. He was a great lover of little children, and a friend to everybody. He knew every little child in the neighborhood.

Under the superintendency of Jonathan Gould, the Sunday-school was in a very flourishing condition; it became the banner Sunday-school in the township, and had a reputation of the very highest order. As a country Sunday-school it is safe to say that it was difficult to find its equal. There were several causes which might be cited to lead to this condition, but one of some importance was the clannish love of home and home ties which pervaded the community. As at country meeting houses generally, the farmers met on Sundays to greet each other, chat a little after church, confer about the plans for work, arrange their brief business affairs with each other, and engage help if needed in their work and for their

Jonathan Gould

business; but the Sunday-school was where the young people met and had their little talks and salutations, and many a love-match was made in the long walks home from the Sunday-school, and these love-matches and the resultant weddings, years afterwards, always turned out well, as was readily attested by the families which grew up from them.

The clannish disposition of the people made them delight in these Sunday assemblings, where they could see so many of their relatives at a single gathering (all in this community were more or less related), and a few words of greeting would leave a lingering pleasure through the following week.

The Sunday-school would be begun with the singing of one of the old Union Hymn-book hymns, reading a chapter in the Bible by the superintendent, prayer, and then the classes with their teachers would read a chapter or two in the Bible, recite the hymns or verses of Scripture which had been "learned by heart," and the blue and red tickets given them for merit. These tickets would be taken in exchange for a Bible or a hymn-book, and many a Bible went into a family for "so many red tickets." Thus the classes were taught by reading the Scriptures, learning the catechism and hymns.

For twenty-one consecutive years Jonathan Gould was superintendent of the Gouldtown Sunday-school, first in the old schoolhouse and then in the new church. He died in 1890, aged 77 years, beloved by his Sunday-school and by the whole neighborhood. Since his retirement from the Sundayschool it has lost nothing in its standing, in fact it has progressed continually. It has at all times had a good library and has had a number of good superintendents and always maintains a corps of good teachers. In the old times there were no lesson-helps, but now every such accessory quickly finds its way to the Gouldtown Sunday-school.

Rev. Theodore Gould

Grandson of Elisha Gould and Great-Grandson of Benjamin Gould, the Founder

Of the family of Elijah and Hannah Murray Gould Rev. Theodore, their son, became the most distinguished. He was born August 12, 1830, and is still living, and at next birthday he will be eighty-three years of age. As a lad he was a studious but sturdy youth; he went to a private school, kept by Miss Eliza Sheppard, but his schooldays were few, for his parents had a large family and it was necessary for him to contribute to their support, which he did, as a boy, by working in a glass factory near his home in Bridgeton.

In 1847, he was converted and united with the Church of his parents — the Gouldtown A. M. E. Church. Four years later he became an exhorter in this church, and two years after this he was licensed to preach and joined the Philadelphia Annual Conference, to which the church at Gouldtown belonged.

Rev. T. Gould, Pastor of Bethel A. M. E. Church, Sixth Street below Pine, Philadelphia, Pa., 1896.

After becoming an itinerant preacher, he was ordained local deacon in the Philadelphia Conference in 1859, being ordained by the then venerable Bishop William Paul Quinn, and was sent to the Danville Circuit, Pennsylvania. Many of the old residents of Danville, Bloomsburg, Wilkes-Barre, Abington Centre, and other Circuit points, remember the work of this earnest and pious young pastor, who travelled one hundred and twenty-five miles to reach all the points of his circuit.

Mr. Gould was then sent to the Princeton, New Jersey, Circuit, which he served from 1860 to 1863, and afterwards was stationed at many points in New Jersey. He was then transferred to the New York Conference, where he filled many appointments. In the New York Conference he ministered to

Bethel Church, Sullivan Street, two years, which were remarkably successful in church progress. After this he was sent to the New England Conference, where he held some of the largest charges, especially the Charles Street Church, Boston, where he served three years most acceptably. He has been twice pastor of Bethel Church, Sixth Street, Philadelphia, the first church organized by the African Methodist Episcopal connection and styled the "Mother Church." He has been appointed Presiding Elder, an office now called District Superintendent, many times.

He was business manager of the Church Publication Department, publisher of the "Christian Recorder," the church paper, and the various other church publications. His management of this department was eminently successful.

The following by the late Bishop B. W. Arnett was published in the Church Budget in 1884 concerning Mr. Gould; "Rev. T. Gould has been in public life for a number of years. He is affable in manner, agreeable in society, honest in his dealing with his fellow-men, a great revivalist, and a consistent Christian gentleman; consecrated to the work of saving souls, exemplary in his life and conversation, the friend of young men, sound in theology and a good preacher."

Mr. Gould was and is a sound business man - a kind so rare among preachers generally. In Bridgeton he owns two dwellings and a store on South Avenue, and a double dwelling on East Commerce Street, besides a farm of about one hundred acres with a fine large farmhouse on the Buckshutem Road, in Gouldtown. He was in the itinerary fifty years and still preaches ably. He is a man of whom his kinfolk in Gouldtown are devotedly proud.

He has three children, Howard, a printer in Philadelphia, Theodore, Jr., an electrician in Boston, and Carrie (Mrs. Albert Rumsey). The last, with her husband, removed this spring from Philadelphia to her father's farm, just alluded to above, where they will supplant a tenant farmer.

Mr. Gould still has one sister living, who is Sarah, widow of Alfred Gould, now eighty-nine years old and residing on her own farm in Gouldtown with her only son, Eugene, and only daughter, Mary, both unmarried.

"Short are the annals of a happy people" wrote Hawthorne. The descendants of Anthony Gould, 1st, son of Benjamin and Ann Gould, are those who came from the daughters "Kitty" and Martha, — that is to say, the children of "Kitty" and Charles Gould, who were Aaron and Anthony, 2nd (Daniel having gone to Massachusetts, and become lost), and the children of "Kitty" and Furman Gould. Of Aaron's descendants there remain Timothy Gould, and his two sons and two daughters, and Aaron Paul and his two sons. Of Anthony's descendants (who was said to have greatly resembled his grandfather, Anthony) there remain the children of his son, William, deceased, and daughters, Phoebe Pierce, still living, the two sons and one daughter of Elizabeth Cuff, deceased, the two sons of Christiana, deceased (Belford and Warner K. Pierce), and the two daughters of Christiana, together with one son, Lewis, and one daughter, Barbara, of Almeda.

The descendants of "Kitty" and Furman Gould, viz.: the sons and daughters of Furman, Jr., Jonathan and Alfred and Charles, 2nd, number a great many. The children of Furman's daughter Martha also left many descendants, but Christiana, who is still living, had no children.

The living representatives of the descendants of Samuel Gould, 1st, are very few, being only those who came through his daughter, Hannah, one of whom is Mrs. Emma Robinson, the wife of Rev. J. H. Robinson, now pastor of Gouldtown, her grandmother being Hannah Gould, who married a Wester; and the children of Hannah's daughters, Hannah Jane, and Caroline, the latter being the wife of Daniel Cuff, of Newark, N. J. Two sons of Hannah Gould Wester reside in Camden County, where they had children, who are now living in New York, Brooklyn, etc. The Rev. Wm. W. Johnson, a minister in the New Jersey A. M. E. Conference, is a son of Hannah Jane, above mentioned.

The surviving descendants of Benjamin Gould, 2nd, were given as up to 1910, in preceding pages. The living descendants of Elisha Gould, 1st, are most distinguished in the persons of his grandson, Rev. Theodore Gould, and his granddaughter, Mrs. Sarah Gould, and their children. There are still other representatives of the families of Furman Gould, in the persons of Albert Gould and William C. Gould, farmers, etc. From these families in their short annals were produced such preachers as Rev. Furman Gould, the first local preacher. Rev. Theodore, as above noted. Rev. James V. Pierce, son of Richard Pierce, 3rd, Rev. Jehu Pierce, son of Jacob Pierce, 1st, Bishop B. F. Lee, a former President of Wilberforce University, Rev. Theophilus Gould Steward, chaplain for many years in the United States army, now Professor of History, French, and Logic in Wilberforce University, Rev. Alex. W. Pierce, of the New York A. M. E. Conference, Rev. Jeremiah H. Pierce, deceased, a member in his lifetime of the New Jersey Conference.

All of these were men of more than ordinary eminence, and those still living are quite distinguished. With the exception of Rev. Jehu Pierce they all came out of the Gouldtown church.

Chapter Fifteen - The People's Patriotism; Ready to Bear Arms for the Country

The people of Gouldtown were not backward to respond to the call of their country. They were early devoted to the cause of American freedom, and heartily hoped for the success of the colonial arms in the War of the Revolution. Three or four out of the community enlisted in the War of the Revolution and served shoulder to shoulder with other Americans during the conflict. Anthony Pierce, Richard Pierce, Adam Pierce, Mark Murray, all served in the Revolution.

There do not appear to have been many of the people of this community in the War of 1812. Furman Gould and a man named Levin Wright — not closely connected with the community — did some service in it; Gould as using his team in conjunction with David Cams' team in hauling supplies to the troops at Cape May. But when the War of the Rebellion came, the young men of Gouldtown made haste to get ready for war. Feeling that the combat just about to open meant the death of slavery, they were more than willing to join in the conflict.

During the presidential campaign of Lincoln, Douglas, Breckenridge and the other candidates, their interest and sympathies were with Lincoln, and seeing and believing that his election meant strife between the North and the South, they were ready at the call. One of the young men of Gouldtown was in Trenton when; Lincoln made the first call for 75,000 troops. This young man hastened to a recruiting officer, enlisted, and was ready to go to the front, but having a physical defect from a broken leg when a boy he could not pass muster.

By means of a copy of Upton's Tactics a company was formed in Gouldtown and drilled. They made the offer to the government to raise a regiment of colored men for the service. Our people remembered the heroic conduct of the black and colored soldiers at the battle of Red Bank during the Revolution, in which they gloried, and they thought to emulate the example of those men. The offer was not accepted, and the people felt such a rebuff that they decided to wait until they were really wanted before again attempting to go to war. So eager, however, were some of them, especially some of the Murrays, that they went as white men and served through the conflict. When colored soldiers were wanted by the government meetings were held at the old schoolhouse and orators came from Fairfield township, offering large bounties for substitutes to volunteer. The young fellows did not feel so much like going to war as they had felt before the rebuff and they informed the orators that they were not going to stop bullets in their places; they would not go as substitutes, but would go on their own footing, which they did when drafted.

Of those who served in the Rebellion were Hosea Pierce, William H. Gould, Wanaca Pierce, Robert Goldsboro, Mark Pierce, Jedediah Pierce, Lewis Murray, William Murray, Ebenezer Murray, Hiram Murray, Lorenzo F. Gould, Charles Lloyd, Charles Pierce, Ephraim Pierce and Henry Murray.

They were represented in the War with Spain by Luther D. Gould, in the regular army, and in the Philippines by Capt. Frank R. Steward, in an Illinois volunteer regiment, and by Othniel Murray, in the regular army, as well as by Chaplain Steward, who was many years in the regular army, and who was government superintendent of schools in the province of Luzon, in the Philippines.

The people of Gouldtown lacked nothing in patriotism from the very earliest period of the government; they were always devoted to their country, their state and their homes; always loved her institutions and delighted to obey her laws. They were not in the war of 1848 — with Mexico; there was no call for their services in this war, but they took keen interest in its progress and General Winfield Scott was their hero. I myself have heard the elderly men of Gouldtown talk of the achievements of General Scott when he was in that war, and I would sit and listen to their reading of the news from the war and hear their talk of the battles of Chepultepec, the storming of Monterey, and the capture of slippery one-legged Santa Anna, the commander of the Mexican Army. They did not side cordially with General Jackson, however, because of his politics.

Chapter Sixteen - Social Life; Some Typical Social Events; Two Golden Weddings; a Social Study

The people of this community were always noted for their hospitality and love of company. In the early days, as well as at the present time, the summer season brought visitors to the place from Philadelphia, New York, and elsewhere, and on Sundays the church would be filled with those anxious to see and meet the visitors to the neighborhood.

Some social events in the neighborhood are here given from clippings from the Bridgeton daily papers as reported at the time of happening which illustrate the social life of the village in those days:

Dinner Party.
At the Home of Stephen S. Steward, Gouldtown

An enjoyable dinner party was given by Stephen S. Steward, at his residence on the Buckshutem road. Covers were laid for ten and dinner served in banquet style, the tables being laden with fried bluefish, stewed chicken, salads, tomato and apple sauce, hot rolls and coffee, followed by cake, ice cream and sugared peaches.

Those present were Mr. and Mrs. Eli Gould, Mr. and Mrs. Lorenzo F. Gould, Mr. and Mrs. William Steward, Mrs. Felts, Mr. and Mrs. Stephen S. Steward, and Chaplain T. G. Steward of Nebraska.

Reminiscences and jokes, with watermelon, finished the evening.

Miss Florence Lee, Miss Edwina Steward, Mrs. Alice S. Felts and Mr. G. A. Steward proved themselves efficient helpers for the occasion.

The Gould Reunion

One hundred and thirty took dinner at the Gould family reunion yesterday, and the Gould descendants were present from the surrounding country, from Salem

County, Camden County, Philadelphia, New York, Boston, Atlantic City, Cape May, Millville, and from the West.

There was an abundance of chicken pot pie, fried chicken, roast meats, etc., and melons, fruit, grapes, and ice cream, and a delightful day and evening were spent. Service took photographs of the group.

Gouldtown, N. J., Items of Interest

The Reunion of the Gould Family A Great Event; Rev. Dr. T. G. Steward the Central Figure

Gouldtown, N. J. (*Special*). Rev. T. G. Steward, Chaplain U. S. Army and son. Captain Frank R. Steward, U. S. Army, attended service at Trinity (A. M. E.) Church. Rev. Mr. Generette, the pastor, preached.

Rev. Dr. Steward will preach to-morrow to the young men of the town and vicinity.

The great family reunion of the Goulds took place at the old homestead, which has been in the possession of this family for nearly two hundred years, inherited from Benjamin and Ann Gould, of which Rev. Dr. Steward is a descendant.

Mrs. Lydia Sheppard, who is ninety-five years of age, and Miss Prudence Gould, are the only two living who are the direct descendants of the above-named couple. Over one hundred and seventy-five were present at the reunion and of this number one hundred and eighteen were direct lineal descendants of the Gould family. They were represented by families as follows:

Oliver Gould and family, Lydia Sheppard and family, Tamson Cuff and family, Jane Webster and family, Abijah Gould and family, Sarah Lee and family, Rebecca Steward and family, Phoebe Gould and family, Clayton Gould and family.

It was a day of rare pleasure and the event was greatly enjoyed by all. The most amusing feature of the afternoon was to see a team of baseball composed of young ladies.

As a whole it was just one of the greatest outings the residents here have ever had. Miss Prudence Gould deserves much credit for the plans of this happy event, at the close of which a picture of all was taken, as a group.

Mr. and Mrs. Rutledge Miller, of Magnolia, N. J., were here attending the reunion.

Mr. and Mrs. Howard Gould, of Philadelphia, attended services at Trinity, Sunday morning.

Miss Lucetta Pierce, who has been for sometime teaching school in Somerville, N. J., will at the opening of the September term teach in Atlantic City, N. J. She is spending her vacation with her mother, Mrs. Anna Pierce.

Gould Family Reunited

Bridgeton, N. J., August 17. The descendants of Benjamin Gould are holding a family reunion to-day at the home of Miss Prudence Gould, near here. Among the descendants present to-day are Bishop Benjamin F. Lee and Chaplain Theophilus G. Steward, of the U. S. A.

Pretty Wedding Occurred To-Day

A very pretty wedding ceremony took place this morning at the residence of Mrs. Alice S. Felts, No. 592 East Commerce Street, when her daughter, Miss Mary Felts, became the bride of Charles S. Dixon, of Boston.

The ceremony was performed by the Rev. Theophilus G. Steward, U.S.A., an uncle of the bride, and the beautiful and impressive ring ceremony was used.

The parlors were crowded by a company of guests, consisting of the bride's uncles, aunts, and cousins, of Gouldtown.

The bride was gowned in a gown the like of which was never seen in this city before, doubtless. It was of the famous Philippine Jusi cloth (pronounced Hoosie) a fine silk. It was the gift of her uncle, the chaplain, who brought it from the Philippines. It was very beautiful, and she carried a fan of sandalwood, brought by her cousin. Captain Frank Steward, from Japan.

The Mendelssohn wedding march was played by Miss Phoebe Felts, a sister. There was no bridesmaid, but the groom's father, John R. Dixon, of Washington, D. C, stood up with his son.

After the congratulations were over a very elaborate wedding breakfast was served.

The happy couple left on the 8.00 p.m. train for Boston, where they will reside.

A Social Study

My mother belonged to a family of seven daughters and two sons, all of whom, excepting herself, lived to advanced age. She died at fifty-seven. Two of her sisters are still living, one having celebrated her one-hundredth birthday October 24, 1909. The other never married, consequently, her age is untellable; but I am sure she is not far from eighty. She has never become an old maid, but has passed her life in deeds of kindness, and is beloved by all.

Eight of the family married and together have had forty-six children, about equally divided between girls and boys. I have the names of all of them before me as I write. Forty-five of these children reached maturity, only one dying before that period — a girl who died at fifteen. Two young men of them left the neighborhood quite early in life and became lost to their relatives. The remaining forty-three are accounted for as follows:

Four died between the ages of thirty and forty (women); three lost their lives by accident, one at sixty-five, one at sixty, and one in his twenties. Two died between forty and fifty; four between fifty and sixty; seven between sixty and seventy; two between seventy and eighty, and twenty-one are still living.

Of the twenty-one now living all are over sixty but one; and five are over seventy. Thus we have a case where eight families had forty-six children, an average of nearly six to the family and reared all of them to maturity, except one girl. Of these forty-six persons, thirty-one of them have lived over sixty years, and, up to the present, ten have passed over the seventieth mark. Not one of the forty-six ever became rich, ever became a drunkard, or a criminal; and no one ever became a pauper or a beggar. To have forty-six children and rear forty-five of them to maturity and to have about three-fourths of them (thirty-one) to pass sixty years is a matter of no little importance; to have this whole body never cost the State a penny either as criminals or paupers is also of some consequence.

Inquiring into the conditions surrounding this group, the first remark to be made is that all the families were poor; but among them was no inherited tendency to disease. In only one family was there the slightest weakness, and it was in precisely this family that the premature death occurred, and that three others died comparatively young. The families were all of sound health and untainted blood. They lived in thinly built, cold houses, dressed poorly, ate coarse food, the meat being chiefly pork, an abundance of vegetables, potatoes, bread and molasses, with plenty of fruit in season, some poultry, fish, and game. They knew nothing of sanitation or hygiene; the boys did rot wear overshoes or overcoats; the girls wore hoods and shawls. Woolen underclothes were seldom worn by the boys. It was no uncommon thing in winter to find snow in our bedrooms as we leaped out of bed shouting and ran through fireless rooms and down-stairs for our jackets, shoes, and stockings. If asked the secret of our power of resistance I should answer thus: first, and best, we had honest fathers and mothers, who married early in life, and gave their offspring the strength of their physical and moral natures. We were not children of broken-down "daddies." Second, we were allowed to eat in the most natural way — all that our appetites required. We were not allowanced, hectored, nor guided; but permitted to obey the wisest mother of all, Nature, within. We ate by instinct until we were satisfied, our mothers attending only to our manners.

So much for the physical. But our social life has also been free. We have kept up a life of considerable fun and frolic; and have not sold our birthright for dollars nor fame. We have lived close to nature. To us plants and trees have their likes and dislikes; horses and cows their morals, and hens vary from suffragettes to queens.

One more fact I must state about these forty-six cousins, forty-five of whom came to maturity and thirty-one having passed sixty, a fact that interferes with much science and philosophy that I have studied, and that fact is this: While all these people are truly Americans of several generations, they are all of mixed European and African descent — they are all colored people.

The total number of this family now known to be alive is two hundred and twenty-five. — Statement written by Rev. T. G. Steward in 1910.

Christmas Memories and Reflections

The return of the Christmas season calls my mind back to the open fireplaces, sometimes smoky; the large wood stoves; the plain chairs and settees which were to be found in the happy homes of my childhood: homes varying but little in their material outline and scarcely at all in their coloring of spirit and manner of expression. Such homes were plentiful three-fourths of a century ago, and the land still abounds with them.

In all of these homes of my childhood, the children were cheerfully welcomed and greeted with joyous words and warm embraces. There were no carpets too good for them to walk on; no chairs too rich for them to sit on; no curtains or linens too fine for them to touch, and as Christmas approached, the sphere of the

Group at Gould Family Reunion

Steward Family. The Six Children of James and Rebecca Steward. Oldest born in 1839. Youngest born in 1847. All living at this time – 1913.

child's liberty greatly expanded. Stories of Kris Kringle (not Santa Claus), and his reindeer and sleigh bells were told to us by Grandmother, Aunt, or Mother, just as real as the love of their hearts could make them.

After long waiting Christmas eve comes; the ground is all white with snow; the big crockery jars are well filled with doughnuts, still warm from the frying and covered down with heavy, clean white cloths that none of their nectar may escape; the red apples are snugly hiding away in their corner in the cellar 'neath their blanket of salt hay; and the mince pies are serenely cooling on the swinging shelf while distant mice grind their teeth with rage. Without may be heard the ring of the sleigh-bells, interrupted occasionally by the report of the overloaded Christmas gun.

The people are not trying to be happy; still less were they going through the solemn silly farce of trying to make themselves or their neighbors believe they were happy. The joy-beams on their faces were genuine scintillations from bounding hearts. Their wants were few; tastes simple, and the slightest manifestation of kindly interest met with liberal responses.

Rev. T. G. Steward, D.D., Chaplain U. S. Army, Retired: Professor of History, Logic and French, Wilberforce University, Ohio.

Christmas morning dawns with its breakfast of sausage and straw-cake, and its flourish of "Christmas presents," of so little cost and of such measureless value. Mother gets a warm hood from laughing daughters who slip it on her head; it has been knit by their own hands in secret; father gets a cap with heavy ear covers, or a warm neck wrap; and the little boys and girls (there were no "kids" in our home) received their presents of useful things silvered over with toy candies. Everywhere on older faces could be seen the reflected halo of a childhood past blending itself with the effulgent light of the reigning hour.

At Christmas time the Child is King, and little ones for a moment rise to a kinship with the divine.

The day broadens and brightens; the boys go gunning or skating; or it may be gather around the stove, crack hickory nuts and walnuts, while girls pop corn or make molasses candy. The dinner just grows into shape amid all this merriment, and is over, the scene changes. The girls bedeck themselves a little more; the boys depart to seek other homes. "Sis's" beau comes, to the disgust of little Johnny, who cannot go out with his big brother. To Johnny, who does not see any sense in "Sis's" having a beau, this halting lump of sleek-headed adolescence is a puzzle. Mary has a different notion, however, and Christmas night is, not infrequently, popping question time. Why shouldn't it be? It is the symbolic season of the union between Heaven and Earth, "a time of love."

As the panorama of my childhood Christmas passes before me I can almost hear the voices commingling from old age to babbling infancy into a chord as uni-colored as the green that cheers the day, proclaiming in tones fountained by hearts divinely touched: "Christmas has returned, let the Heavens rejoice; Christmas has returned, let the Earth be glad." And as the mantling canopy of benevolence extends itself from the distant past covering my track of three score years and more, and the present year with all its myriads glides under its folds, there comes to me the sweet murmurings from trustful humanity; "God is love." "It is good to be here." Our tabernacle is already builded, and we dwell with Him Imanuel. With us Christ is not only born but abides; one of us, **one with us,** through the possession of generations in their career through the ages.

Two Notable Family Events: Golden Weddings of Brother and Sister

Mr. Eli Gould and Wife, Mary Steward Gould, Celebrate Fiftieth Wedding Anniversary

Fifty years ago last Saturday, Eli Gould and Mary Steward were married at the home of the bride's parents, Mr. and Mrs. James Steward, at the Steward Farm on the Millville turnpike. That was March 12, 1860. Last Saturday, the fiftieth anniversary of that event — their golden wedding — was celebrated at their home on Burlington Avenue. The festivities were from three until eight p.m. Though the day was a most inclement one, nearly a hundred of their relatives and friends responded to the invitation to make merry with them and a very enjoyable gathering it was made. Besides those of their friends about the neighborhood, there were guests from Salem, Millville, Philadelphia, and elsewhere, and remembrances from relatives in New York and Boston.

Mr. and Mrs. Gould both trace their ancestry back to the earliest Colonial times, and have always resided in this community. The Goulds and Pierces practically constitute one family and the gathering on Saturday showed a good many of their names. There was an abundance of good cheer, the most "spirited" of which was plain orangeade. The tables were set for dinner before nightfall, and between the time of nine o'clock, six tables of about sixteen persons each were served with chicken salad, fried oysters, sandwiches, oranges, cakes, Neapolitan ice cream, coffee and tea. Very nearly one hundred persons were served. Principal among those present were Dr. G. T. Watkins, pastor of the bride and groom, Chaplain T. G. Steward, brother of the bride, and Bishop B. F. Lee, a cousin of the bride, and the bride's only two living aunts, Mrs. Lydia Sheppard of Millville, who was one hundred years old last October, and Miss Prudence F. Gould, Mrs. Sheppard's sister.

Many beautiful presents were received by the couple including, in part, a solid gold thimble and a pair of solid gold cuff-buttons from Mr. and Mrs. William P. Almond, of Philadelphia; a five-dollar gold coin from Chaplain Steward, a comb, handkerchiefs, and handkerchief basket from Mrs. Steward, eleven $2.50 gold coins from different guests, and a one-dollar gold coin from Miss Prudence Gould, currency from Mrs. Frank Pierce, Mrs. Hattie Pierce, Mrs. R. M. Seeley, and others, and large picture in gilt from Mrs. Phoebe White, of Philadelphia, and berry spoon, cold-meat fork, gold-lined ladles, glass berry dishes, fruit dishes, celery dishes, cake dishes, bread plates in many varieties, rich and beautiful table-cloths, linen napkins, water pitcher, Japanese teapot with cream pitcher and sugar bowl, and many other articles and "gold" clock from Mr. Howard Gould, of Philadelphia.

Mrs. William Steward

The table was decorated with gold ribbons extending from an artificial lake in the center of the table to the ceiling of the dining-room. The lake was surrounded with smilax interspersed with water lilies, and in its center were two columns represented by two large glass vases filled with daisies, between which was suspended a large gilt "50"; about the lake were golden candlesticks, altogether making a very pretty effect. The lake itself was a large mirror laid upon the table. As the guests entered the house a little wedding bell was pinned on each one by an attendant.

Among those present were Eli Gould, the groom, Mary Steward Gould, the bride, Dr. George T. Watkins, their pastor. Chaplain T. G. Steward, L. F. Gould and wife, Stephen S. Steward and wife, William Steward and wife, Mrs. Alice S. Felts, brothers and sisters of the bride; Bishop B. F. Lee, Eugene Gould, Miss Mary Gould, Misses Lizzie and Emma Stewart, William Cuff, Mrs. Mary Pierce and Miss

Helen Pierce of Salem; Mrs. Lydia Sheppard and son, Thomas, of Millville, and Mrs. Sheppard's granddaughter, Mrs. Lydia Sheppard, II, of Haddonfield, Mr. and Mrs. Ernest Sheppard of Millville, Mrs. Alice Almond and Mrs. Phoebe White of Philadelphia, Howard Gould, of Philadelphia, Mr. and Mrs. Joseph B. Stewart, James Pierce and wife, James Wynder and wife, Murray Wynder and wife, William B. Gould and wife, Mr. and Mrs. Harold Pierce, Mrs. Harriet Pierce, Mr. and Mrs. Menon Gould, Mrs. Ephraim Pierce, Miss Lizzie Cato, Miss Prudence Gould, Miss Clara Steward, Miss Madeline Gould, Mrs. Ella Pierce, Miss Dora Pierce, Miss Constance Gould, Mr. and Mrs. Frederick Steward, Miss Edwina Steward, Mr. and Mrs. Leslie Gould, Mr. and Mrs. Edgar Gould, Mr. Oscar Pierce, Eli Gould, Jr., Miss Inez Gould, Herschel Gould, Mrs. Lizzie Gould, Miss Jeanette Gould, Miss Marie Gould, Miss Helen Gould, Miss Lucetta Pierce, Miss Nellie Goldsboro, William Goldsboro, Mrs. Harriet Goldsboro, Mrs. Mary Chase Beckett, of Holmesburg, Pa., Walter Hubbard, Samuel Lively and wife, Miss Maggie Felts and some others, whose names were not secured.

Jacob Wright and Wife

Chaplain Steward in an address said: "This is my first opportunity to attend a golden wedding and although this put me to considerable trouble and expense, I could not afford to miss it. There are in this community four or five other people who have lived out their half-century, but have not celebrated it. Our good brother and sister have seen fit to celebrate theirs and invite us to join them. It is an event that ought to be celebrated. When two people have lived together fifty years and have thus set an example for the stability of family life, they have a right to announce the fact and their friends do well to congratulate them. On behalf of the whole community I tender to this couple my congratulations. As a community we are not speechmakers, but I am sure we can all join in the expression of our high appreciation of this example of solid family life."

With some other pleasantries he concluded his address with wishing both bride and groom continued health and prosperity.

Mrs. Gould then in a few words thanked their friends for the kind response to their invitations and also for their generous help in making the entertainment so successful.

Another Golden Wedding: Mr. and Mrs. William Steward Married Fifty Years

Many guests were present; happy occasion at their home at East Bridgeton; large number of beautiful and useful gifts received

Mr. and Mrs. William Steward celebrated the fiftieth anniversary of their marriage last Saturday, at their home at East Bridgeton. The exact anniversary occurred last Monday, but as a matter of convenience the Golden Wedding was held on Saturday. The hours were from three to ten o'clock and many of their relatives and friends called during that time to tender their congratulations and join in the festivities of the occasion. Among the guests were Mr. and Mrs. Eli Gould, the latter Mr. Steward's sister, who celebrated their golden wedding over a year ago. Mr. Steward has two brothers and three sisters, the youngest or "baby" of the six being sixty-two years old. The house was decorated with flowers, the profusion of golden-glow being especially appropriate and many crimson ramblers adding their beauty. Music was furnished at intervals by Misses Phoebe Felts, Constance Gould, Mildred Pierce, and Harold Pierce, on piano and violin, and there was also some vocal music. A collation was served of sandwiches, chicken salad, olives, coffee, Neapolitan block ice cream, and cake. An elaborately iced wedding cake adorned the table.

Many beautiful gifts were received. Among those who sent congratulations and remembrances were the following: Mrs. Sarah Gould and Miss Mary Gould, Dresden celery dish; Rev. and Mrs. M. M. Middleton, salad bowl; Mr. and Mrs. Reuben Cuff, gold thimble and fountain pen; Miss Edwina Steward, salad bowl; Mr. and Mrs. W. W. Hubbell, of Brooklyn, bonbon dish; Mr. and Mrs. Ernest Sheppard, Dresden and gold mustard cup; W. L. Evans, salad bowl; Mrs. Anna and Miss Lucette Pierce, silver cream ladle; Mrs. George F. Bundy, of Philadelphia, gold belt buckle; Mrs. Jane C. Pierce, gold-lined bonbon dish; Mr. and Mrs. Charles F. Dixon, West Somerville, bonbon spoon; Captain and Mrs. William Jerrell, cut-glass berry-bowl; Miss N. P. Elmer, handkerchief box; Mr. and Mrs. Walter Durisoe, of Philadelphia, bonbon plate; Mr. and Mrs. Harold Pierce, drawn-work centerpiece; Misses Lizzie and Emma Stewart, embroidered towel and watch fob; Mr. and Mrs. Roy Pierce, tumblers; Miss Albertine Felts, Somerville, Mass., congratulation card; Mrs. Phoebe White, Philadelphia, gold cuff-buttons, Mrs. Mary Almond, Philadelphia, brooch; Mrs. J. L. Titus, New Brunswick, cuff-buttons and brooch; Rev. and Mrs. Theodore Gould, gold-lined olive-spoon; Mr. and Mrs. Calvin Pierce, berry spoon; Mrs. S. Maria Steward, M.D., of Wilberforce, Ohio, three handkerchiefs, collar, and gold comb; Mr. and Mrs. Eli Lee, meat fork, William A. Cuff and family, cuff-buttons; employees of the Pioneer, gold-lined table spoons;

Publisher, gold clock; Miss Lizzie Cato, gold-lined teaspoons, Mr. and Mrs. Belford Pierce, salad fork.

Gold and silver coin and notes: Mr. and Mrs. Edgar Gould, Thomas J. Sheppard and family, of Millville; Mrs. Alice and Miss Agnes Gould, Mr. and Mrs. Warren Pierce; Chaplain T. E. Steward, of Wilberforce, Ohio; Mr. and Mrs. Edward Pierce, of Washington, D. C; Stephen S. Steward, Mr. and Mrs. Howard W. Jerrell, Mr. and Mrs. Menon Gould, Mrs. Rebecca and Miss Pierce, of Philadelphia; Mr. and Mrs. Eli Gould, Mr. and Mrs. Leslie Gould, Mr. and Mrs. Ambrose Russell, of Pittsburgh; Mrs. Alice S. Felts and family; Miss Ethel M. Pierce, of Longport; Miss Susanna Pierce, Mrs. Lydia Sheppard, Mrs. Hortense Klose, of Philadelphia; Mr. and Mrs. James R. Pierce; Miss Prudence F. Gould, Mr. and Mrs. B. F. Pierce.

The celebration of two "Golden Weddings" in the same family, as were the two which have been here related, is of very rare occurrence; yet in Gouldtown there have been several golden weddings passed without general recognition. Jacob Wright (whose mother was a Pierce) and his wife, Anna Gould Wright, passed their sixty-ninth wedding anniversary.

Chapter Seventeen - Educational Facilities of the Neighborhood

In the colonial times in which the early population of this community lived, it is not to be supposed that the facilities for education were very common. The people, however, even in those times, endeavored to give their offspring the rudiments of learning. They were mostly taught to read and to write, with some idea of calculation. The Presbyterians connected with the "Old Stone Church" in Fairfield, then generally called New Englandtown, took active interest in giving aid to schooling the children throughout Fairfield township, in which Gouldtown was situated. At a very early day a schoolhouse was erected on property belonging to a Hosea Shaw on the road leading "from Gouldtown to Bumbridge," where a pay school was kept, for many years, previous to 1800.

Here the early Goulds, Pierces, and Murrays, together with the Westcotts, Batemans, Fullers, and others got their schooling. This schoolhouse was about a mile from the residence of Benjamin Gould, 1st. About two and a half miles northward from this ancient Gouldtown schoolhouse was another called the Lummis schoolhouse. Here the Lummises, Bowens, Woodruffs, Parvins, and Garrisons went to school, but the schoolhouse that those from

Gouldtown and others nearer "Bumbridge" attended was the one standing on the Shaw property. Who or of what character the teachers were who taught here has not been recorded. In 1807, on January 8th, Hosea Shaw and Rachel, his wife, made a deed for the "School house and lot of land" (the metes and bounds being given), "containing one hundred and thirty-five square perches" to "Robert Hood, James Hood, James Westcott, Peter Sleesman, Robert McGee, and Ephraim McGee, for the sum of One Dollar." The deed does not say that the schoolhouse and lot sold to those men was for school purposes, but it seems to be self-evident that they were trustees of the school. The deed simply conveys the property to them and their heirs and assigns, but the consideration being but One Dollar is proof it was not for their own personal use.

Absalom Wilson, School Teacher

Robert Hood resided on the farm on Reeves Road now owned by the brothers Servais, and Peter Sleesman resided on the farm about a quarter of a mile north of the present Gouldtown church, lately owned by Nathanial H. Atkinson. James Hood probably resided with Robert Hood, but later moved into Bridgeton. Peter Sleesman afterward moved into Bridgeton also, and by his will left one thousand dollars for the schools of Bridgeton; the sum being still invested and the interest paid to the school fund of Bridgeton. Westcott, and the McGees, resided near Fairton.

In 1809 Isaac W. Crane, a young and brilliant but later rather eccentric lawyer, came from Salem and settled in Bridgeton, where he practised law for thirty years; during this time he found leisure to teach school in this schoolhouse where the Goulds attended. He was a tall, fine-looking man and was always called "Lawyer" Crane. When teaching school he endeavored to get the Goulds to make suit for what he alleged to be, by right, their inheritance in the Fenwick and Adams estates, but they would have nothing to do with the proposition.

The Academy on Bank Street, Bridgeton, was erected in 1795-1797 and incorporated by a joint stock company. The names of the stockholders and incorporators, which were those of the best and most prominent citizens of the town, are recorded with the articles of incorporation in the Cumberland County Clerk's office, dated in 1797. So liberal were the incorporators with their educational facilities that a number of the young men of Gouldtown attended school there in the years following, and long before the building of the Bank Street public schoolhouse; among those so attending from Gouldtown were Enoch Gould, who became a carpenter and builder, Abijah Gould (3rd), James Steward, Freeman Gould, Anthony Gould (2nd) and others. [10]

Gouldtown School House

As was previously stated, the Gouldtown school was under the moral direction of Presbyterians; the old Gouldtowners being inclined to that denomination and attended the "Old Stone Church." The old women of the locality have many a time related how they walked the long distance on Sundays from Gouldtown to that church, when they were young. For better accommodation, a small frame church (also used for a school) was built northward of Gouldtown, before alluded to as the Lummis schoolhouse, on the road leading from Gouldtown to Deerfield at the intersection of what is now the road to Carmel. Becoming dissatisfied with the arrangement, the people of Gouldtown in 1823 purchased the Westcott school building, at the same time securing the lot where the Gouldtown schoolhouse is now located, and moved the building upon it.

This lot, comprising one acre, belonged to the estate of Elisha Gould, youngest son of Benjamin Gould, 1st, and in the division of his estate was a part set off to. Lydia, his daughter. She had married Archibald Cuff, and, for the sum of four dollars, they made a deed dated March 13, 1823, to Anthony Pierce, 2nd, Jesse Gould, Reuben Pierce (son of Anthony), Elijah Gould (son of Elisha) , and Daniel Siro, Trustees, to them and their successors in office, for school purposes. On this spot the school of Gouldtown has ever since been.

In this schoolhouse many teachers have taught school. Among them were Jeremiah Sayre, Nathaniel Bateman of Fairfield, Josiah Bennett of Fairton; Jeremiah Carll, Hiram Carll from Deerfield; three of the daughters of Benjamin Gould (2nd), one of whom, Miss Prudence Gould, is still living. Absalom Wilson of Salem, his brother Charles Wilson, and still another brother Reuben, and David Cuff — all of Salem. Horace Bishop of Herring Row, who was a favorite teacher of that generation; Seth Husted, Albino Davis, and James Barrett of Shiloh, — all these taught in the little old one-story schoolhouse; Benjamin T. Bright and B. W. Rogers were the last who taught in it. Since then the teachers have been many; instead of one there have been two, one down-stairs and one up-stairs. The old Board of three or five trustees has been legislated out of office, the schools being now school district No. 1, under the Fairfield Township school board, with always one or two members from Gouldtown on it.

A Teacher Fourteen Years

Recollections of Gouldtown and Vicinity in Fourteen Years

The writer, B. W. Rogers, was called upon about the year 1866, by Mr. Benjamin Bright, to finish out his term as teacher in the Gouldtown school, as Mr. Bright wanted to start a grocery store on Commerce Street near the bridge. It was a new business to me, teaching school, and Mr. Bright had to do some coaxing to get me to go, but I soon became so well pleased with the job that, with the exception of two winter terms which I taught at the Loder School, I remained at the Gouldtown School nearly fourteen years.

The old schoolhouse was one story and no vestibule, and very annoying it was if children came late, when

Bentley W. Rogers, School Teacher, and Retired Capitalist.

removing their wraps and putting up their dinner kettles in the schoolroom. It was hard on the teacher; and besides there were no grades; all in the same room from *a b c* up to algebra; but I got along and the children liked me and I liked them.

The opening exercises consisted of singing, reading a chapter in the Bible, and most of the time I had an organ to help with the music, and it gave pleasure all around; and I must say that these years of school teaching were the happiest in my life. There were many things very unpleasant for the teacher, of course, but my heart was in the work, and besides I had a good set of trustees who stood by me and they saw I was trying to do my very best to get the children to learn; if any were unruly and had to be corrected, and the parents complained to the trustees, they passed it by, — knowing as they did, that in nine cases out of ten the correction was proper. I shall always think kindly and have respect for the memory of these men; Mr. Abijah Gould, Mr. Andrew Gould, and Mr. Holmes Pierce who were trustees most of the time.

Horace Bishop, School Teacher

About the year 1871 or 1872 the city of Bridgeton was induced to give five hundred dollars, and Fairfield township to give a like amount, and they employed Mr. Enoch Gould to remodel the old schoolhouse, put on another story and eight feet in front for a vestibule. Mr. Gould did a good job and anyone else would have charged at least twelve hundred or fifteen hundred dollars.

Mr. Enoch Gould could do more work in one day than any man in Gouldtown, and it is said that he was known to walk two or three miles out, when he had no carpenter work in winter and cut his two or three cords of wood per day; Mr. Gould was about one-quarter Indian. It is said that he was a hustler at anything he went at. He raised quite a family and lived near the schoolhouse. All his children were well-behaved and they had a good mother to instruct them, and what I say of this family I can truthfully say of many other families in Gouldtown — they were God-fearing and honest in their dealings and transactions, and remarkable for their hospitality. One winter I taught a singing-school, and on Thursday evening did not go home, but stayed with some near-by family to supper, and the invitations were two and three weeks ahead for me to take supper at their house — I shall never forget their kindness of heart.

In looking back some thirty-five years, I can tell of some very severe winters and the snow and ice and difficulty of getting to and from school. One winter I remember was an icy one and the boys would skate along the pike just as on a mill-pond; I was overturned in my sleigh once going to school, and my dinner spilled out in the snow. Once the old schoolhouse got on fire and such a scampering to get out you never saw! It was in the roof, and was soon put out with a few buckets of water. If the many born and raised in Gouldtown could be brought back again, the population of the place would amount to twenty or thirty thousand, for go whore you will, you can always find someone raised in Gouldtown.

Yes, they were happy times and I wish I could have them over again; but it cannot be, and sooner or later I too shall be gone to the "Land beyond the River" to join the loved ones gone before.

I must not forget to mention my good wife and the service she rendered in hearing the younger ones recite in their classes, and if she was absent, then I had the assistance of some of the older scholars and to them I was greatly indebted. Some of the names I recall were Mary Pierce, Mary Gould, Josephine Gould, Miss Pierce, daughter of Mrs. Phoebe Pierce, and others. I may also mention the fact that during the fourteen years I got up fourteen exhibitions and every one was a success. The money received from two of them was used for a library. Anyone familiar with the vast amount of work getting up an exhibition must realize that my heart was in the work, and that it was one of the bright spots in my life. I must give due credit to the scholars: some in particular like Rev. Isaac Showel, Rev. Alex. Pierce, Holmes Pierce, Jr., Paul Gould, Josephine Gould, Mary Gould, Anna Gould, Hannah Gould, Dorothy Gould, Anson Gould, Samuel Gould, Harriet Gould, and others; I cannot recall their names now.

Favorable mention should be made of the distinguished talent turned out from Gouldtown, such as Bishop Lee, Chaplain Steward, Rev. Theodore Gould, Dr. Jesse Gould, Rev. Jeremiah Pierce, Rev. Isaac Showel, Rev. Alex. Pierce, and a few other names not recalled.

The natural soil of the place is first class for crops of any kind, and the climate is delightful.

        Respectfully,   B. W. Rogers.

Mr. Rogers is a retired capitalist of ample fortune, and wealthy at the time of teaching school, as he has described; his wife, who assisted him, was a woman of culture; and Benjamin Bright, whom he succeeded, was a man of some wealth also, his father having left him an estate of eighty thousand dollars. He was for many years an active and energetic member of the Bridgeton Board of Education and a prominent citizen. He is now deceased.

Those school teachers did not receive the almost princely (in comparison) salaries now paid to instructors, even in the rural districts. Captain Jeremiah Carll, who was captain of a sloop in summer months, walked to and from the school, a distance of five miles daily, kept school from eight o'clock in the morning until four o'clock in the afternoon, with one hour intermission at noon, and for this service he received about thirty-five dollars a month. School was also kept every other Saturday, but on those Saturdays it "let out" a half hour earlier at night. Albino Davis walked from his home in Shiloh — three miles west of Bridgeton — to Gouldtown — a full five and a half miles, and taught school the same number of hours daily, and received the same pay. Horace Bishop taught many winters. He was the beloved teacher of those who attended the Gouldtown school sixty years ago; he drove a horse and sulky, sometimes a buggy, from his home in Herring Row, two miles below Fairton, and he got no more salary than the others. Absalom Wilson and several others boarded in the neighborhood.

There were singing-schools also in those days. The first teacher of "singing by note" in Gouldtown was Alphonso Sumner, a colored barber. He would walk from Bridgeton to the home of James Steward, and here he would meet a class of children and young people, and put them through the do-re-mi, the breves and semibreves, the "Scotland's Burning," the crescendo and diminuendo to the fullest extent. He was a good teacher of the rudiments of music. Professor Collister Morton, a peripatetic music-teacher, who had a circuit of singing-schools from Cedarville to Deerfield, gave one night a week to a Gouldtown class, who were as much delighted to hear his "fiddle" lead the strains and give the pitch as they were to learn music from his teaching.

There was no choir in the Gouldtown church until after the erection of the new church in 1860; since then they have always had a choir, with organ, in both the church and the Sunday-school; and there have been graduates from the Gouldtown school attending the South Jersey Institute, in both voice culture and instrumental music. There are now good pianists and violinists, as well as good singers, among the Gouldtown people. The first female school-teacher in Gouldtown was Mrs. Sarah Lee, mother of Bishop B. F. Lee. Then her sister, Mrs. Rebecca Steward, taught one or two summers. Then Miss Prudence Gould, another sister. Mrs. Enoch Gould kept the school one or two summers. Miss Anna Hoover, of Millville, and Miss Emma Sink, of Fairton, were also teachers several summers.

[10] The Bank Street Academy was built jointly by individual stockholders and Brearly Lodge No. 9, A. F. & A. M. under the following ancient agreement, made one hundred and twenty years ago in February, nineteen hundred and thirteen, on file in the County Clerk's Office of Cumberland County:

"Memorandum of an agreement entered into and agreed upon by each and every of the subscribers each one severally and individually of the one part with the others jointly of the other part, as followeth, viz.:

"1. It is mutually agreed that the subscribers hereto shall form themselves into a society for the promotion of Literature agreeably to an act of the Legislature in such case made and provided.

"2. In order to carry the designs of this institution in full and complete effect, it is agreed that suitable buildings for the reception of scholars be immediately erected.

"3. Whereas, the members of Brearly Lodge No. 9 have proposed and made the following offer, to wit: That they will be at the one-third part of the whole expense of erecting and enclosing a building of forty feet by twenty-two, two stories high, with a cellar under the same and two chimneys and two floors laid, and in the same proportion to bear the expense of painting the outside and the putting up of a lightning rod, and of enclosing the lot, and of paying and bearing in the same proportion in all needful and necessary repairs to the said building which may hereafter arise — the windows in the lower story excepted — and also to make the stairway out of the lower story to the upper at their sole and entire expense;

"And whereas the said proposal will not only lessen the expense of erecting said building on the part of the subscribers but will add ornament and beauty to the same, it is hereby agreed that the same be accepted.

"4. That the said building be erected on a lot given by John Moore White, Esq., for the purpose, and that the lower story of the house be appropriated to the use of a school or other purposes as the majority of the subscribers present at their stated meetings shall agree, except the entry which shall be for the joint use of the subscribers and the members of the said Lodge; that the subscribers shall occupy the whole cellar except that part which shall be under the library room, and that the members of said Lodge shall, at all times and forever hereafter, have the sole use and occupation of the upper story upon the terms and conditions aforesaid, and it is hereby understood and agreed that each party shall be at the expense of completing and finishing the stairs by them respectively to be occupied at their own expense, except as is before excepted.

"5. The costs and expenses of building and finishing said house on the part of the subscribers hereto shall be divided into one hundred equal shares or parts and each subscriber to pay in proportion to the number of shares he subscribes.

"6. That if the whole number of shares are not subscribed by the third day of March next that then and in such case the unsubscribed shares shall be divided into as many shares as are subscribed and each subscriber shall take the residue in proportion to the shares by him subscribed.

"7. That on the said third day of March the subscribers shall meet at the new store house, opposite the store of Seeley and Merseilles, at six o'clock in the afternoon of said day and appoint a committee who shall have full power and authority to erect and build said house in conjunction with a committee to be appointed by the Lodge upon the terms and conditions aforesaid, and for that purpose the said committee are hereby authorized to make contracts and do all needful and necessary things for the purposes contemplatetl by the subscribers hereto; to receive all moneys which may be subscribed and pay out the same as occasion may require, and that it is the meaning of the subscribers that the said committee proceed to complete the building in such manner as they shall think best for the interest and advantage of the subscribers and without any further meeting of the said subscribers unless a majority of said committee deem it proper and call a meeting accordingly.

"9. That no subscriber shall transfer any of the shares by him subscribed until all shares are subscribed.

"10. That all persons holding a share or shares by transfer shall be entitled to the same privileges as the original subscribers have and enjoy.

"11. That the subscribers shall be entitled to vote in proportion to the number of shares they hold at the time of voting.

"12, That each subscriber shall pay on each share by him subscribed the sum of Four Dollars on the first day of April next and the sum of Three Dollars on the first day of June following and the remainder, if any, as soon as called for after the house is completed.

"Done at Bridgeton, February 21st, 1797."

The subscribers, whose names are recorded, were:

John Moore White	Eden Merseilles	Charles Howell
Davro Seeley	Jajees Burch	Abel Randolph
Enoch Book	Abel Corson	Clarence Mulford
Enos Johnson	Jonathan Holmes	Mosheck Sapp
Ebenezer Seeiey	John Pierson	Ephraim Seeley
Abraham Satre	Mark Riley	Manoah Lummis
Zachariah Lawrence	Reuben Pierson	Nathan Middleton
Jonas Keen	Davto Potter, Jr.	Eli Elaier
Jeremiah Buck	John Brown	John Woodruff
Reuben Burgin	John Mulford	Walter Robinson
Robert Smith	James Giles	Joel Zapp
Smith Bowen	Josiah Parvin	John Irelan
Joseph High	Benj. Champneys	

The entire 100 shares were subscribed by them.

Chapter Eighteen - Some Literary Efforts of Gouldtown Youth Thirty and Fifty Years Ago

These are offered — not because of their merit — to indicate a literary taste in the community. It is thought, however, that these examples are not altogether without merit. They could be increased by many such specimens which are to be found in the neighborhood.

The chapters which follow are taken at random, from a story written and published in a newspaper many years ago, and indicate clearly the habit and thought of this community two or three generations earlier. The people at that time had very pronounced notions of propriety, morality, religion; and were independent though considerate to others, in expressing and impressing their own opinions and predilections. It may be said here, that the hero of the story was Hezekiah Gould, the son of Jesse Gould, the carpenter and housebuilder. Hezekiah learned the trade with his father, but he was a very energetic and ambitious youth, with a positive genius for mechanical investigation. After completing his trade he became a machinist and ranked with the best in the city of Bridgeton in this trade. His career has been before mentioned. The heroine was the girl he married. Both were mulattoes, but were pictured as black (for obvious reasons at that time) by the author.

John Blye: Or Trials and Triumphs of a Whitewasher's Son

By "Will," Author of "The Gem of the Alley," etc.

After supper the family, with their guests, returned to the parlor. The old folks — that is, Mr. and Mrs. Blye and Mrs. Voulons — entered into a general conversation, which dwindled down to personal reminiscences. Mrs. Voulons informed her host and hostess that she was a Pennsylvanian by birth and ancestry — that her progenitors had lived among the quiet Quakers for several generations, but that her husband was a West Indian of French extraction.

Somehow or other young folks will get together, no matter how bashful they are, and by this time John was getting along first rate with Miss Eteline; and though they sat a little apart from the old folks, they were quite close together themselves — possibly so that the noise of their conversation might not disturb their parents — and laughing and chatting like old school mates.

"Please don't call me 'Mr.,' just call me 'John.'"

"Well, 'John,' then," said Eteline, "are you fond of music?"

"Yes, I am very fond of vocal music."

"Do you sing?"

"Oh, no, indeed. I wish I could!"

"But you play, I suppose?"

"Not well, I have taken some lessons on the piano, but you know you can't have the advantages of professional teachers here that people in the large cities have."

"Your instrument is a very nice one."

"Yes; won't you favor us with a song?"

"Oh, my!" smiling archly, "I am an Episcopalian, and the songs I would sing might be too naughty for Methodist ears."

"If you are a Christian you will not sing what you ought not to sing," said John, gravely.

"There, now, I did not mean to wound you with my leArity. Of course I am a Christian — a member of the High Church. But which is your church?"

"We are Methodists," said John.

"Then I'll have a chance to go to a new church. Will you have time to show me around town any while we are here?"

"I will try to. The evenings are moonlight now, and perhaps you and your mamma would like to visit the iron works and the glass works in the evening. We often go and look in on them. It is a very pretty sight to see the red, molten iron, and the sparks flying and the great engines puffing and wheezing; and at the glass works to see the red globes of glass being blown out into large cylinders for window panes, or dropped into the moulds and blown out into jars, bottles, goblets, etc."

"Oh, yes, I would like to go. I am fond of moonlight walks anyhow. Do you have any parties or social gatherings?"

"Not much. There are but few colored families in this town, and they are mostly poor, hard working people, and have but little time for recreation."

"What do you do then — just go to workshops days and to prayer-meetings evenings, eh?"

"We don't have theatres and operas as you do in the city, so we take up the time in reading and studying."

"Oh, now you are chiding our city doings. Now you had better cease. I won't have you finding fault with our city amusements, so there now!"

"I was not finding fault with them; I don't like them, though, and I don't think they are any good in the world!"

"Don't think they are any good in the world! Only hark at you! Why, what would we do without the fine, classic music of the great masters as rendered by the most wonderfully endowed artists at the operas." And the wonderful imaginative genius of the great play writers would be the merest drudgery to read if it were not for the theatres. Such things are good; they stimulate and bring out the latent or half awakened powers of human exertion."

"Oh well, now, I am not going to argue the matter with you. Anything that is bad can't be good, and I have yet to be convinced that society is any better by having theatres and such things than it would be without them. Of course I don't know anything about them — hope I never shall; but you do, and if I undertake to argue with you, you'll get the better of me.'?

"That's because your side is weak. But I don't go to theatres and operas. Mamma is very strict in that regard. It is not fashionable in Philadelphia for colored people to go to such places. Only the low and vulgar go, for the better class do not like to be insulted as they would be by the whites, if they should go. They are not allowed to enter the same part of the house with white ladies and gentlemen, but are put aside with the lowest classes of low whites."

"Well, I suppose the colored people don't own any of them, so they can't say much. The theatres belong to the whites, and I am satisfied they shall have them; but I fear you will become lonesome in our silent village and soon want to be going back to Philadelphia."

"Oh, no, indeed. I see you have some rare books to me, and I was saying to Mamma awhile since that I should have a rich feast in perusing them. I am so fond of reading."

John went to bed that night with a new sensation in his heart. The evening's conversation with Eteline and her mother, enlivened as it had been with some choice songs by Eteline, who had a really fine voice of good culture, had awakened a fluttering that was new to him.

Eteline was pretty, of majestic form, elegant carriage, educated and refined, and entirely different from the kind of girls of his own race with whom he had hitherto associated. She was evidently of aristocratic breeding according to John's notions, and he felt himself exalted beyond measure by the notice he had received from the young lady, and her mother.

The next day John found himself hastening home from his work with a little more than his usual eagerness, and the next it would have been plain to any one in the secret that there was an attraction to impel him homeward after the close of his day's labor.

Ah, John, the *sturdiest* boy has a weak spot when he gets to be about your age, but go on; the bird that flutters and warbles before your eyes is worth catching. Only be careful that you make yourself worthy of the prize!

"Mr. Needles," said Absalom Wheeler, while John was rather absently comparing a pattern with his draught, "I am convinced that boy can't put up this engine an' run it."

"Who, John? Why not?"

"Cause he's too young and inexperienced for one thing, and then he's careless and lazy. Why, I have to watch him like a cat would a mouse all the time for fear he'll get something wrong."

"Does he ever get anything wrong?"

"No, but I don't know where he would go to if he was let go on. I measure and try every piece of the machinery to be sure that no mistake is made."

"I am glad you do so; it will be all the better for John as well as be a further assurance that everything is right."

"Oh, I mean to have every thing put up right, for I expect I shall have her to run, and I want her to run like a top."

"I believe it is Mr. Holloway's intention to have John to run her. He has always taken a great interest in him, and I guess almost considers him as one of his family. I think John is a very smart boy and of remarkable genius. It is seldom you meet with a boy of his years who has so steady a head on his shoulders. I believe Dr. Holloway's sister, little Teeny Holloway, has given a good deal of her personal attention to his education, and is very much attached to him."

"Well, they're a gay couple, I'm sure! She's as ugly as the pillar of salt, and John's as black as Egypt's darkness. Well, I don't believe he'll ever run that engine, that's all. I don't believe it's in 'im."

"We'll see after we get her up," said Mr. Needles, turning away.

"Yes, we will see. John Blye nor no other black Blye shall run that engine while my head's hot," muttered Absalom.

"John's very young, but my! I've seen several boys running engines and making good engineers, who were no older than John, and hadn't near his theoretical knowledge. I am glad Absalom has been such a friend to him, though. It has been well for John, and it has been well for Absalom, for I've never seen him so careful and exact before," said Mr. Needles to himself.

That was Saturday, and the men were allowed to "knock off" earlier on Saturdays than on the other days of the week, and in addition to stopping work at three o'clock, now, Mr. Needles told John he could have two or three days off the next week, as the moulders were up with the pattern makers, and the machinists had to wait for some brasses.

John was glad of this, and began to lay off a good time for himself with Miss Eteline and her mother.

There were several places to visit of more or less importance in the rural districts as well as some families upon whom they should call, and he hastened home to acquaint his mother of his plans for entertaining their guests and to enlist her cooperation.

As he neared his residence, Eteline was standing upon the piazza, and commenced calling out to him —

"Oh, John, I've been on an exploring expedition — a voyage of discovery — to-day, and I've found just the sweetest place where you must take mamma and me to-morrow."

"To-morrow! To-morrow is the Sabbath, and we should not take pleasure excursions on the Sabbath," said John, smilingly.

"Oh, dear, I wish I had been brought up a Puritan, then I would always have my thoughts about me, too," said Eteline, with pleasant gaiety.

"Do you approve of such things?" asked John.

"As Puritans? Certainly I do, only I'm glad they're all dead," replied Eteline, laughing.

"Oh, pshaw! No. I mean Sunday walks for pleasure," said John.

"Generally I don't. Mostly I think they are real naughty," said Eteline with mock gravity. Sunday walks or week day walks are rarely pleasure walks to me, but a Sunday walk, to-morrow, will be pleasant, because you will go, and to balance the thing I shall take my prayer-book and whenever you show any signs of jollity I shall read you 'Gloria in Excelsis.'"

"I have something better than that to tell you," said John. "I shall not be at work three days next week, and I hope to spend a good deal of time with you."

"Oh, that's nice! I won't say anything more about going to-morrow, only I hope it will rain all day, now, so we won't have to go to church and I'll have you to laugh and talk to all day," said Eteline.

John felt as if his head was getting wrong side about or something. What could Eteline mean by saying a walk would be pleasant because he would go and what could she mean by wanting to-morrow to be a rainy day so she could have him all day to laugh and talk to? Was she in earnest or was she only joking him to make him feel flattered? Fie, fie, it was nonsense to believe that Etehne Voulons, the rich city lady, should think anything of him, — only to pass away the time while she was away from her gay city circle. What was he, compared to the brilliant and polished gentleman who followed in her train when at home. He would banish all nonsensical thoughts — that he would, for she would soon return to the city and he would be forgotten!

"Mamma," said Eteline, as they retired to their chamber that night, "the longer we stay here the better I like it. I am surprised and delighted beyond expression to find such culture and refinement among people of our own race."

"Yes, daughter, it is a delightful satisfaction. These people, no doubt, had a very humble beginning and they are very modest still, but without any sycophantic fawning. What we see here is genuine gentility, and I am pleased, my dear, that you find pleasure in staying here," said Mrs. Voulons.

"Indeed I do, mamma. Mr. Blye is one of those men who can be characterized as of solid worth, and Mrs. Blye's intelligence is of that common-sense sort that I could wish myself possessed of," said Eteline.

"Mrs. Blye is a lady whose character, habits and piety I am sure can well be emulated. Though always serene and happy, she tells me that she has known sorrow and has passed through the fires of affliction. Of five babes she buried four, and only one — John — has been spared to her, and, like your poor mother, my Eteline, her struggles have ever been to guard against making an idol of her boy," said Mrs. Voulons, feelingly.

Eteline came to her mother's side and putting her arms about her neck with tender caress she kissed her cheek and brow with sincere affection, saying,

"John Blye is much more worthy of being idolized than your worthless daughter, and I think my own mamma's piety, and habits, and character are as worthy of emulation as any saint's on earth."

"You are partial, my dear, and cannot see your mother's shortcomings."

"No, because she has none. I think my mamma and papa are the best people in the whole wide world; and the nearest people like them are Mr. and Mrs. Blye," said Eteline.

"Do not form your opinions too quickly; sometimes appearances are deceptive, but it is a very high mark of excellence that these people have worked their way from modest beginnings up to a position of respect and comparative wealth," said Mrs. Voulons.

"I suppose we shall accompany the family to their church to-morrow, shall we not, mamma?"

"Yes, we will go with them. I do not approve of worshipping with their denomination, but if our desire to worship God and reverence His name be sincere it matters little what may be the denomination with which we worship, and we must also accord their opinions the same respect we shall want for our own," said Mrs. Voulons.

The next day was the Sabbath and quite a sensation was manifested in the Methodist church when two elegantly attired and strange looking black ladies were noticed with the Blyes at the services, as it did not turn out to be a rainy day.

Another Chapter from "John Blye."

John wasted no time over Absalom, who had regained his feet boiling over with rage. A half dozen men had got between him and Dr. Holloway and prevented any further assault by either. Dr. Holloway was paying no attention to him. Pointing to the wedge, John said:

"This accounts for all the trouble. The wedge that belongs there has been removed, and another inserted for the purpose of throwing the machinery out of line. I do not wonder it would not run, but it is astonishing I did not discover it sooner."

"Do you think that was done purposely to prevent the engine's running?"

"Yes, it could not be for any other purpose," said John, proceeding to unscrew the bolts and remove the wedge.

Absalom had by this time left the mills in a great rage not to return, so we will dismiss him here.

Removing the wedge, John began a search for the one that belonged there. Going to a rude "cupboard" where Absalom kept his towel, soap, hair brush, etc., he found it wrapped up in stout paper.

After the adjustment of the machinery again, which occupied an hour or two, steam was turned on, the engine started, and everything worked with the precision and nicety of its former action.

The facts of the matter had by this time become known among the employees and John became the hero of the mills, while indignation was loud and strong against the absent Absalom.

Anyone in the village after that having anything to say against John Blye — the engineer, was advised to "sing it small" as his friends soon numbered the entire population of the place.

But events of a more stirring nature began to agitate both the home of Dr. Holloway and the little village of Edgefield.

The first event was the marriage of Dr. Holloway and Miss Grace Harris. This can as well be imagined as described. It came off during the Christmas holiday season and of course was the event.

Girls are singular things, and when they "take a notion," they will have their own way and carry out that "notion." There is nothing a woman cannot do when she has once determined she will, for with her it is preeminently true that "where there is a will there is a way."

Teeny Holloway had determined to have Miss Eteline Voulons at this wedding, for during Eteline's visit at the Blyes she had made many friends; by her elegant manners and the intelligence of her conversation as well as by her warm and sympathetic heart, she had won the esteem of all with whom she had become acquainted.

In addition to a formal card, Teeny had sent a personal letter urging her to come down, coupled with one from Mrs. Blye. The result of this was that Eteline's commanding form was seen among the gay guests at the home of Judge Harris on the wedding day. She was not alone, for the young engineer, John Blye, was also an honored guest. As has been before intimated, John's musical abilities were considerable and he was not unaccustomed to mingling with the best social circle of the place, so his presence among the guests occasioned no surprise — unless it was among those from neighboring towns.

The festivities passed off happily. The great event was over, and Dr. Holloway and his young bride settled down like sensible folk in their new home, settling themselves to making each other happy.

As the winter drew on towards spring a dark and sombre foreboding began to shadow the land.

"I'll bet there'll be a war yet," said some, while others laughed and said, "They ought never to let 'Old Abe' take the Presidential chair."

Ominous misgivings were rife in the nation during the whole winter, but when, at last, Abraham Lincoln arrived in Washington from the growing and buoyant West, and was peaceably inaugurated President of the United States, the people breathed freer and began to feel that the prospective trouble had passed over.

This feeling was soon, however, dispelled. Fort Sumter was fired upon at last, two months and two days after the firing upon the "Star of the West," off the city of Charleston.

The Southerners, maddened at first by the John Brown raid in October, 1859, looked upon the turn of affairs as the culmination of Abolition aspirations. The sound of the drum began to be heard all over the land. Volunteers were called for and preparations warlike began to be made. A few months rolled by and the whole nation is plunged into a bloody civil war.

Even the little town of Edgefield shared in the general excitement. The shrill scream of the fife, and the roll of the drum called up the loyal villagers, and the "squad" was soon drilled and ready to march to the front. Soon the mills and the fields began to be depleted of laborers. "Call" after "call" for volunteers to supply the sinews of war was made by the President.

New life began to be infused into the wheels of industry. Contractors, speculators, "shoddy mills" and greenbacks soon became known, and men pocketed fortunes of the Nation's wealth in a day.

John worked steadily at the mills for a while, but at length a new industry sprang up at the Eagle Works. The government wanted iron bedsteads for the soldiers, and iron latches and hasps for transportation chests, etc. The Eagle Works had secured a "contract," and new machinery to be made. The lumber business had fallen off at Edgefield, and John's services being in so much demand at the works, the saw-mills were stopped — the laborers going to war — and John was given the important position of assistant to the engineer-in-chief, Mr. Needles. Nearly two years had elapsed since John had exposed Absalom Wheeler's trick at the Edgefield mills, and so signally defeated the plan so cunningly laid to prevent his running the engine. During all that time of John's trial and mortification, Mr. Needles' confidence in him had never failed, and when John's triumph came, Mr. Needles' satisfaction was intense.

Still came the calls for "three hundred thousand volunteers." Recruiting officers were in every hamlet, visiting every store, office and workshop. One day the Hon. Mr. ___ a member of the Legislature of John's native State, visited the Eagle Works, recruiting volunteers for a State regiment. While talking eloquently to a knot of mechanics, some of whom had already given him their names, one of the men said, "Here's Mr. Blye, let him go, too."

The honorable recruiter, with gushing loyalty for his country and exaltation for the soldier, replied:

"Yes, if I had my way he might go along; if I had my way black men should go along to carry you boys' guns and water cans, and wait on you and black up your shoes, and you should do nothing but march and fight."

John was a general favorite, respected and beloved by every man in the works, and at these remarks the men said no more but hung their heads in shame — shame for the man who did not know their John, and shame for their state and country which made it possible for the utterance of such remarks with all they might imply, and one by one they slunk away to their work.

But at last came the Proclamation of Emancipation — then came calls for enlistment of the contrabands and freedmen and finally calls for colored volunteers all over the country.

Spring Bottom shared in the new excitement. Like magic, almost, strange colored recruiting officers appeared in the hamlet, and soon here and there a blue suit and blue cap appeared in the streets.

The war fever seized upon John also; but he did not like the idea of going to war for his state or country as a mere hireling. He was perfectly willing to go to war as a state volunteer, for he felt that to go any other way would be an acknowledgment on his part that he was not a citizen of a state. Spring Bottom raised a pretty strong club of stay-at-homes under the hireling rule of the government, declaring they would not go to war unless they could be accredited as volunteers to the state to which they belonged. John joined this club and was elected captain of it. The more the drums beat to arms the more anxious were its members to go to war. At length so urgent became the colored people of that and the adjoining counties to go to war, and so popular had John become among his own people that he was induced to take the initiatory steps towards raising a regiment. The success in this undertaking was so promising that, at the instigation of some of the leading colored men he wrote the following letter to the Secretary of War:

"Hon. Edwin M. Stanton, Sec. of War, Washington, D. C.

"Sir: I have the honor to inquire if a regiment of black men would be accepted by the War Department and credited to this State; and, if its officers of black men would be commissioned to command it as are the volunteer officers of other volunteer regiments, with the same pay and rations for privates and officers.

"Very respectfully, John Blye."

This letter was endorsed at the War Department "John Blye, Esq., of [Gouldtown, N. J.] makes inquiries concerning raising a colored regiment," and returned with the following letter:

"War Dept., Washington, D. C, 1863.

"Sir: The government accepts the services of colored men as United States Colored Troops. They are allowed a compensation of $6.00 per month for privates and $8.00 per month for non-commissioned officers. *It is not deemed advisable to allow colored men to command.* I have the honor to be

"Very respectfully,   A. A. G. [12]

The result of this correspondence was to disband the various clubs that had been organized, the men declaring they would wait for a draft and see if the government would draft those whom it would not recognize as citizens.

Soon, however, came the clarion voice of glorious old Massachusetts, and the country remembers yet what she said.

John at once determined to become a Massachusetts soldier.

[11] An actual occurrence, the remarks being made by the Hon. P. L., now dead, in the presence of "Will." Instead of the words "black men," however, the word that was used may be guessed.

[12] This correspondence, in substance, was an actual occurrence and the letters are *verbatim et literatim.*

Chapter Nineteen - A Story in Blank Verse

In Stowe Creek township, near Flax landing on Stowe Creek about a century ago stood a brick house. It still stands there and, though modernized, is now owned by either Frank Ridgeway, or the estate of Captain Miller. It was said to have been erected in Colonial times, and the tradition, in early days was that it was the rendezvous of pirates; and was finally made the prison of a fair captive of the pirate chief. Seventy-five years ago the natives used to call it "Joe Compton's Haunted House," because nobody would live in it.

(The following story, in blank verse, was founded upon this legend, by a Gouldtown boy, then about 20 years old, and who is still living. The name of the writer is assumed, and this same boy wrote many things in prose and verse under assumed names, one of which, as I now remember was "Ichabod."

This story of "Luilla" was written about 1860.

Luilla: The Corsair's Victim.
A Tale of South Jersey by "Oliver Tweedle."

I'll tell the tale, as it was told to me;
But yet, to 'hellish with a little grace,
Must weave in fancy; for it would not do
To give it in the rough with no carving -
For meats are always better with seas'ning;
In earlier times, 'tis said, wild daring men.
Devoid of fear of law, or punishment
For crime, t' increase their wealth would band themselves,
And choose a chieftain whom they would obey:
A sharp, sagacious, cunning man 'twould be,
Most apt, and young, and handsome, too, to boot,
With good address; one who could probe right well
The gentleman; could visit the abodes
Of wealth — to mingle with the high and gay;
To be the greatest sport in sporting scenes,
To be the most solemn where things devout
Are wont to be enacted, and to pry
The inmost secrets of the haunts of wealth
And find the, to his band, most harmless way
To possess it and to escape, uncaught;
And this while being the admired of all
Admirers, and the star of all who gaze.
And deeds by such were done that froze the blood;
Deeds of plunder that would end in murder.
And sometimes worse than murder, — death outright
Is better oft than torture to compel
The victim to disclose some secret place
Where wealth and plunder might be stored away;
Or, some fair victim, who, by luckless fate
Had fallen in their power, to be forced
To yield her virtue to th' unhallowed care
Of such men-monsters; — so much had I learned
Before my narrator, an aged man.
Began his story in this wise, to wit:
"Jean Paul Retour was born, no matter where.
It might be France, or Spain or Italy,
In some large city or a country town;
He might have been a duke's son or a clown's, —
It matters not, his younger days I knew
But little of, nor care I more to learn.
'Twas in his early manhood that I knew
Aught of him, and to know him then was but
To love and to admire and to revere;
For he was grand and noble, good and true.
His own descent would count for nothing, for
His own proud blood could found a family;
Tall, upright was his form, and conscious pride
Of his own person gleamed forth from his eye.
His raven hair in curling locks hung o'er
The square and lofty shoulders; and the brow
Was high and haughty, and the jet black eyes
Showed nought of fear of danger seen or not;
The straight, thin, well-set and transparent nose
Showed restlessness of disposition, and

The small square chin and thin compressing lips
Showed cruel firmness in a purpose set -
And he was handsome, aye! surpassing all;
No door was closed to him, but all were glad
To win his smile, and gain a passing word,
But, ah! a spell hangs o'er him and would break
In vengeance! — Foul crimes had been committed
And murders done that baffled inquiry.
Merchants and banks were robbed by one Pedro,
'Twas said, a bandit with a bandit band;
And church and convent shared alike their fate.
And all attempts of sheriffs, high or low.
To trap the desperadoes were in vain.
For none could tell, or give a clue where might
Be found the hiding place of band so bold;
And other robberies, and murder e'en.
Had been committed where 'twas thought that ev'n
The bold Pedro could not have found the scene.
At last a man was robbed and left as dead,
A merchant he with stores of golden coin
Locked in his house secure, with double bolts,
And all his family gone to while the time
Of evening at theatre or church;
But he, well knowing where his treasure was.
Remained to guard as 'twere, and if perchance
A passing friend should enter, to beguile

In pleasant talk the lonesome hours away.
The time would be well spent in sweet converse.
Jean Paul did enter, welcomed ev'rywhere,
A no less welcome did he now receive,
With adroit skill he plied his host with words,
About the fair Ilene or bold Henri;
With artless queries learned he that they
With all the servants, save one — Olao
Had gone to seek amusement, or devote
An hour to worship. How a fire did gleam
From the black eye of Jean, as Olao
With tray of viands rich entered the room
And placing them upon a table paused,
As if to hear command; his eye did meet
The hurried gaze of Jean for one instant, —
It was enough, a magic spark had caught
The tinder sleeping in his own gray eyes
It blazed and lashed itself into a flame;
Demons held carnival therein as if
A scheme t' increase their demoniacal joy
In dreadful orgies were consummated.
And Olao smiled; his very soul shone out
In frightful blackness through his vicious eyes;
He placed himself behind his master's seat
And said, "My Lord, the viands, see, are here
For you and for your noble friend, and I,
Your slave, am here to do your bidding; and

The wine will loose your brain and make your thoughts
More free."
    One, two, and yet another glass
Was quaffed, Jean rose as if to go, but stayed;
Then quick as thought a dagger pierced the breast
Of the rich merchant and he fell to earth.
"He dies!" said Paul, with one triumphal look,
"Olao, at the spoil, or else the herd
Of sniffling women will be here and then
The clue is given e'er we could escape."
One last look as he left the house Paul gave
To see that life had left the body, and
No tales were likely to be told of him.
He looked too hasty — for, when he had gone
And faithless Olao had followed him,
The bleeding man revived, and to the crowd
Assembled cried: "It was Jean Paul Retour,
He's the bold bandit Pedro, and his band
Are Jean Paul's men," and closed his eyes and died.

It was a subterranean chamber where
Were congregated many stalwart men,
Each clustering round a common centre
Paying deference to a manly form
Who had just entered, who recounted low
An adventure. List, now! a spring is touched,
Another form admitted; 'tis a maid
Or vixen, as you will; her look was wild
And agitated, and she paused as if
She feared to break the silence.
                    "Speak, hussy!"
Said a thundering voice from out the crowd,
And stepping nearer to the bending form
Of him who seemed to be the chief, she said
"Pedro, my chief, you did your work too soon.
For he, your dagger pierced, died not until
He had revealed your name; so have a care
How that you mingle in the throng of men.
They'll seek your life — for now they'll know who 'tis
That leads the band of Pedro."
                    'Twas midnight!
The dim light of the tapers shone athwart
The corridors; the massive pews of that
Great church: its holy furniture showed dark
And rich in the dull glare of taper light.
Its beautiful images, and the robes
Of absent priests, melted and modified
The scene, and there amid the tapestry
That overhung the image of Mary,
The Mother of our Lord, knelt the fair form
Of woman, and a step was heard close by.
She started up, a dagger met her gaze,
"Luilla," said a voice she knew full well.
And joy and gladness lighted up her face,
"'Tis you, my only love," she feebly said,
"For you I've prayed the Virgin all the night,
Now tell me — "but the dagger," and she fell
Pale, trembling to the ground —
                    "Was pointed at
The heart of any found who would tell tales,"
Said Pedro, for 'twas he, and as he raised

The drooping girl, repeated in her ear,
"I cannot strike the heart of one like you,
Nor can I trust you out among the world;
I am a robber chief, but not so bold
As put my neck within the halter noose,
So you'll away with me."
    "**No,** strike me dead!
Take, take the bloody hand I blindly loved
And slay me here, I am prepared to die,
For nought is stronger than a woman's love
But her despair," — thus said the stricken girl
In accents weak.
    The robber chief would not.
But bore her off unto his den of thieves.
And thought by words of flattery to win
Again the love that lived but once and died.
He swore by the "Lord George" she should be his.
And that by her consent, for if he would,
Could he not break her to his will, for she
Was in his pow'r, what could she do but yield."

Canto II.

Sometimes such bold, wild, daring, reckless men
Found helpmates for their profit, who would share
Their plunder, on the sea; who were as bold
In crime as they, and cared no more for laws
Of men or nations, or a higher pow'r.
'Twas well sometimes to ship his spoils away.
So Pedro thought, to sell in other climes.
So he had leagued himself with pirates too.
And they with each exchanged their ill-got goods.
And profited thereby; — a rendezvous
For both their gangs was made, to seek ashore:
The sea beats madly 'gainst the broken rocks
And dashes its white foam amid the clouds
And roars and surges like a giant bound
And bound it is; the tow'ring rocks above
Stay its proud waves, they can no farther go;
A ship at anchor in the distance shows
By the wan gleam of starlight, and the crew
Pull a small boat towards the breaking shore
Where none but madmen dare to risk their lives;
But at the helm a swearing steersman sits
Who knows the path — has traversed it before,
And safely runs the boat to a small light
High up the cliff. The boatmen give a sharp,
Short whistle, and a door springs open wide:
A sentry stands, the password now is given,
A scaling ladder falls into the boat.
And captain, crew, and plunder soon are safe
Within the den so cunningly devised.

An inn, a common country inn, along
A sparsely traveled road, 'tween no great towns,
Is filled with country folk — a brawling set.

Who for amusement congregate to spend
An hour or two in drinking and in chat,
And high their humor runs; and loud uproar
Is mixed with vulgar laughter.
                    But a hush —
The scene is stilled — a new arrival's made:
A coach and 'tendants fill the open space
In front the house; a tall and graceful man
Alights, bearing the seraph form of one,
Who seems to be a maiden lost in grief.
For ever and anon a sigh escapes,
But the veiled features are not let to view.
And slapping his fat thighs brave Loraine says:
"Ha! Pedro, now I have it, well you know
That I will aid you, if I can, to 'scape
And take your dainty cargo with you, too, —
I know a port where none as yet do come
To lade their ships, but where I have e'er this
Unladen mine of gold and buried it,
Now go you there, since this is not the place
For you to stay, and spend a quiet life,
What say you. Eh?"
            "I say I will away
To any place where I may but possess
This object of my passion."
                    "The New World
Is then your home."
            Then springing to his feet
Pedro called out: "Ten men of you I want.
By lot, to be the agents of a man.
Unknown; to guard his wealth, tenant his lands,
And build a mansion house for him when he
Shall come to hold them; and again I want
Two others, but by choice, to guard a charge
That I shall give them — Alberto, your wife,
And you, I shall make use of for this trust
And Irish Bill, a better is not found."
It was a motley crowd — from verdant youth
To hoar age the lot impartial took;
I'll not describe them all, but merely tell
Of the main agents, who were chosen out:
Orlando Conara, a dashing youth.
Was first appointed over all the rest,
And they must do his bidding as they would
Were he their chief; in faith, a gallant chief
He'd make, his tall, commanding form and mien
Showed he was not of common parentage.
The keeper of the house is all aglow
With smiles and blandishments, the gaping crowd
Bow and cringe, and give way to the pair,
Who, as the landlord says, "are shown their room,"
And then indulge in comments; some one says.
"He is a bridegroom with his dainty bride,
Spending a honeymoon." And others say
"She is his sister and they two have met
A sad bereavement, for did you not see
How sad he looked and how she seemed to sigh?"
But Piano, the old steward, put in his voice
And said: "It is the Maestro, he who owns

The house and lands and all that here surrounds.
He comes and goes whenever 'tis his will,
And none dare question him, but I do think
As Albro says, 'tis a young bride who now
Accomp'nies him" —
        You know the man, my friend,
I do not doubt, and know the maiden too,
'Tis none but Pedro and the Luilla,
And Pedro's men compose th' attending train.
We will not follow through the vaulted way
Long leading from the chamber where they go
Unto the den; but meet them there amid
The scenes of revelry.
        An hundred lamps
Illume a spacious hall well thronged with men.
And women too are there and not a few,
And strains of music fill the smothered air.
A table groans with viands and repast
Of richest odors show a sumptuous feast
Is ready for some honor'ble event;
The pirate chief and robber chief discuss
A topic strong and stronger cup of wine.
Yet so it was; a helpmate he possessed,
Who outvied him in hideous, horrid looks —
A short and crumpled, humpbacked thing was she,
I cannot call her woman, nor do I
Believe that she was woman; for a fiend
Would be most likely to put on her shape.
Her chin was sharp as any eagle's beak
Yet blunted off; her mouth from ear to ear
Encircled half her head, which dev'lish thing
Sat squattily between the humpy things
She called her shoulders and two other things
She called her back and breast, I wonder not
That such a face had such a hooked nose,
Or such green eyes matched such red, grizzly hair.
Now "Irish Bill" in turn deserves a glance;
Although not prominent, he holds a place
In the selected comp'ny, which must care
For the selected charge.
        A short spare man,
Of light but withy form, and sinewy
Was he, with skinny face that wrinkled up
From chin to brow when but he chanced to smile
Or speak, or even wink his eyes, which orbs
Were large and full, protruding from their seats
Like any hare's, but which he could not help;
His hair of yellow hue was short and curled.
And when he spoke a spasm seemed to jerk
His entire frame — his lungs would fill and heave
And vi'lent splutter make, as from his mouth
His thick and smothered voice found utterance.
I said the other nine were common men.
And it was so; but one deserves a space
Of notice. Diff'rent from the rest in hue.

Yellow and curling were his massy locks
And mild and placid was his sky-blue eye,
A ready smile awaited all who chose
To address him; courteous and polite,
He was cut out and stamped a gentleman.
But now and then a quick electric flash
Shot from those placid orbs; the quick expanse
And flutter of that thin, straight waxen nose,
And hasty motion of the head and hand.
The constant watchfulness, all tend to show
That there is something lurking still within.
No wonder is it that the like of him
Is found in such a band — 'tis just his place,
The other men were nought but common men.
Of various dispositions, as you'll find,
In any comp'ny; but Albertero —
Alberto and his wife were two, the like
Of whom I think 'tis very hard to find:
Tall was the man and gaunt and sinewy,
With grayish hair and straight and lank the locks.
And sunken eyes of piercing, stinging black.
And hollow cheeks with yellow, wrinkled skin;
A deep mouth reaching well around and filled
With snags of teeth, with eyeteeth long and sharp;
A broad, flat chin with stubbed beard beclad —
Like frost just oozing from the glazier's mouth.
And nose of three-inch measure, full and hooked
The end, to keep the superficial curve -
And 'tis the truth, my friend, he looked more fit
To be companion for the wildest apes
And ogres too, of largest size, to stay
The dread and terror that's inspired by him,
Than be companion of the womankind.

Reclining calmly on the deck, Pedro
Watched with the pirate captain every move,
And seemed to study with his strongest will
To weigh her thoughts, divine her inmost heart.
And he succeeded, too, somewhat, 'twould seem,
For turning to the pirate in a tone
Of mingled bitterness and joy, he said,
'Fairest of all the fair ones is my bride
That is to be, — yet 'tis the greatest crime
That I've committed thus to bear her off
From friends and kindred and a pleasant home.
To share the fortunes of a wretch like me —
In faith my heart reproves me more for this
Than plunging my stiletto in the heart
Of my best friend. Does she not look, Loraine,
Like some fair goddess weeping o'er the fate
Of some fair protégé? If I could but
Induce the girl to overlook my crimes
And see that they were necessary, then
She might forget her past life and her home,
And bow to fate before it breaks her."
"You'd
Break her, then," said Loraine, "or bends she not?"
"By heaven! she's mine, I'll do just what I will!"
And a low chuckle glided o'er the sea.

Canto III.

Days, weeks, and months successive pass away.
But still Luilla's home is on the sea,
But not in the same ship she started with;
For Pedro showed his skill so much the first
Attack upon an unarmed merchantman
That Loraine did divide his stock of war.
Some heavy guns and small arms without stint.
With him, and fitted up the captured ship
For chasing harmless prizes, and the crew
That was found in her had their choice to swear
Allegiance to Pedro or drink the deep.
Some turb'lent ones, of course, were murdered straight,
For they might give him trouble, and perhaps
Might cut his throat if they became too strong
By numbers joining to them.
              Thus Pedro,
Augmented by his twelve disciples, who
Were chosen by the lot to do his will —
Became a corsair bold, and dreaded much
By shipping merchants in full many ports.
Cinara was his mate and quite as bold.
And Hilo Maenon was his cabin steward
And he with Albertero and his wife.
Old Zaniffe, had the charge of Luilla,
Who, in a private cabin fitted up
With great luxuriance and artful taste,
Was closely guarded — though it seemed not so.
For he, the wily corsair, would not seem
To govern harshly, nor e'en would he seem
To hold her is. his ship as with his will —
But fain would make her think with fluent words,
He, of necessity, a virtue makes.
How that the changes came, it is not need
That I should tell you, Sir, but come they did.
And Conara received instructions full
To follow out the plans by Loraine laid
For Pedro's guidance ere they parted ships.
And as you do not know them, I will tell
In what they did consist in my own way.
But quite at home among them, and they seemed
To pay deference even to him, like
As if he had some trait that would command
Respect — and so he had, for though his skin
Was black as night, true brav'ry dwelt beneath.
As well they knew in many plund'ring scenes.
Of Afric's ebon race he was a son —
And well might Afric pride herself to own
A son so noble in his form and mien:
His name was Hilo Maenon, and the lot
Had chose him with the rest.
              The night drew on
To morning and the feast was well-nigh done,
The pirate and the bandit chief had made
Their plans, quick work must now be done to move
The bandits' necessary stores unto
The anchored ship as yet the morning light

Lingered and danced not o'er the rippling wave, —
Great chests, and heavy, filled the lab'ring boats,
As to and from the ship the sturdy tars
Bent their strong oars; and stores of merchandise
Of best and finest quality, the spoil
Appropriated from some wealthy son
Of commerce. But we next will turn our eyes
To Pedro, who, unconscious of the noise
And bustle, seems to be absorbed within
Himself, and thus he muses: "I'll become
A corsair, too, for lucky have I been
On land; I've heaped up gold and silver bright —
Yon chests contain my treasures, all but one;
I'll be a corsair and I will possess
That other one — she can't escape me now;
The sky and sea shall be our boundaries,
The ship our home — I'll win her to myself,
And when those fellows do perform their work,
I'll bear her to my mansion where the past
Will be forgotten — but if she resist
My wiles of love, what's left me then to do?
Nor will she either, for she loved me once.
And what has been can well be o'er again;
I'll soothe and caress her with gentle words.
And make her love me by her own proud will."
The morning sun beheld the gallant ship

Swift driving o'er the blue — no trace of land
Was visible; the sporting flying-fish
Darted across her bow in multitudes.
And ever and anon a screaming bird
Hovered o'erhead awhile, then hied away;
The gentle breeze crested the distant wave
And swelled the canvas of the lab'ring ship;
It moaned and sighed amid the loose cordage,
And fanned the cheek of Luilla, my friend, —
For she was there and leaning o'er the waists
Look'd into the deep sea and thought of home,
And friends, and childhood's early scenes, I think;
Her mass and pray'r, her spir'tual adviser —
Of all she loved and all she thought lov'd her —
Ah, then, the tears unbidden 'gan to flow;
The breeze now playing with her ringlets black
That cluster o'er her snowy shoulders, and
Her crimson cheeks receive the kisses light
Of the majestic sun. A form she stands
Of unsurpassed beauty, e'en among
The fairest daughters of the sons of men.
Her fragile form is gently rocked and swayed
By the soft motion of the sailing ship;
One waxlike hand the ships gunwale supports
The other grasps her cherished rosarie.

In South New Jersey e'en unto this day
There is a weird place where many tales

Are told of Bluebeard, once a pirate, too.
And money holes abound in plenty, where
'Twas said that he had buried stores of gold
And anxious diggers searched with hushed voice,
To gain the treasure, which, 'twas often said
Was heard to rattle 'neath the cov'ring stone;
And many vouched when they had digged a ways,
They found the iron chest which held the prize.
But being so o'ercome with dreadful awe,
They spoke! and down the chest immediate sunk —
For 'twas a legend that old Bluebeard called
A stalwart stripling from his pirate crew,
More wicked than the rest and steep'd in crime,
And charged him thus: "Son of the sulph'rous pit,
Seest thou this gold? I leave it now to thee,
To guard until I do return — Dost hear?
See that thou guard'st it well; and if perchance
The hand of man should seek and find, the fiends
Of hell in their black arts assist to guard!
And if a human voice dost hear, raise all
The powers of hell to bear it off. Spirits
Of darkness keep their vigils near to thee!"
A charmed bullet pierced the young man's brain.
He died while standing upright; yet no mark
Or wound, 'twas said, was seen; they buried first
The gold, then stood the corpse upright upon
The chest, then filled the pit and laid a great
Flat stone upon it.
      This Bluebeard was none
But Loraine, pirate of the Southern Seas;
He found the place; a quiet, sheltered cove,
A few miles up the Bay of Delaware,
Had landed many times and stored his spoils,
Among a band of servile padders, who
Inhabited the country and by stealth
Surreptitious conveyed them to the town
Of Quakers, where they might be sold for coin.
This is the place of which Loraine had told,
Jean Paul Retour the night he left the den
And he had made his plan to this effect, -
That Conara and his associates
Should seize upon the land as best they could,
And build a mansion house and till the soil
And keep communication with the town
Of Penn, from whence to import luxuries,
And thus to make a home adapted to
A foreign lord and lady when they came.
And so it was; a beautiful abode
Was finished with the most exquisite taste,
And flow'rs and forest trees adorned the lawn
Which stretched expansive from the edifice;
And carriage-drives, well gravelled and laid off,
And shaded by the tow'ring oak and pine —

In truth it was a home that would invite
The most fastidious, for the corsair gave
Command that no expense be spared to make
His home full worthy of his bride.
                        Three years
Were passed — the time drew near at which
He said he should be done of robbing ships —
And should forsake the deep and land his prize,
And enter in the social walks of life
And as exiled nobleman from lands
Where prisoners of state were forced to leave
Their home and kindred — was thus much his plan.
"And now, my friend," my narrator kept on,
"We must return our thoughts unto the ship, —
Plunging and ploughing through the restless main,
A thing of beauty, she, a thing of life.
And freighted with the spoils of many lands.
Of captured ships the burthen, and her decks
Were always trimmed for action. Pedro knew
'Twas better to prevent confusion than
To cure th' effects by losing in the fight.
Thus was the home of Luilla, but not
Of Luilla alone; for merchantmen
Oft carried passengers of female sex,
And so it chanced that Pedro had run down
And taken a rich commerce ship of France,
With two French ladies who became his spoil —
For any one he thought to be of use
He failed to put on shore at liberty
But pressed them to his service; so it was

With those two ladies; he had reckoned well
That Luilla desired company
Of her own sex; how to provide for her
And not endanger his designs had been
A subject often pondered in his mind.
Not that he feared she could escape from him,
Or any plots she might with comp'ny make
Would foil the least his foul intentions, for
He knew she was secure, such trusty guards,
Were Albertero and his old hag wife —
But he did fear the slightest counterpoise
Would alien her affections; to this end
Was strict forbiddance made for any one
Save the old guards and Maenon, the black steward.
To hold converse or say a word to her.
It happened lucky then, so Pedro thought,
That these two maidens spoke another tongue —
So henceforth were they her associates.
Their names were Lizzette and Enfronica,
And Lizzette bore a striking likeness to
The fair Luilla, so much so that one
With slighting gaze would not the difference tell.
The only 'stinguishment between the two
Was in their hair — Lizzette's was golden hue.
The night was dark and stormy and the wind
In fitful howls swept through the taut cordage;
The good ship rocked and swayed before the gale
Now upon beams, now bows beneath the waves.

Onward she hastens, glad, she seems to near
A port at last, so tossed and beat by seas
Her oaken sides delight themselves to find
A harbor is before; with sturdy ribs
They check and dash the billows back upon
Their own revengeful heads.
                    The quiet Bay
Of Delaware is seen athwart her prow;
The surging sea is stayed at last, the calm
Smooth waters of the Creek of Stowe
Bear on their bosom Paul Retour's proud ship
And through the murky night a friendly beam
Starts from a watchful signal-light hard by
And signal answers signal; by the ship
The cables run, the good ship winds around.
At last she ceases in her progress, rests -
From years of weary toil she rests at last!"

In the poem there follows the description of the life in the Haunted House, referred to previously.

Chapter Twenty - Some Present Real Estate Possessions of the Inhabitants of Gouldtown

The Western extremity of Gouldtown extends to Southeast Avenue at the corner of Pamphylia Avenue, in the second ward of the city of Bridgeton, New Jersey. At this point is the home of William C. Gould, a descendant of Rev. Furman Gould. His wife is Elizabeth, daughter of George Pierce of Salem. She is a descendant of Menon Pierce, 1st, of Gouldtown. This home of William C. Gould consists of a farm of twenty acres, which he inherited from his father, Furman Gould, 2nd. It extends eastward along Pamphylia Avenue until it joins an eleven-acre lot belonging to Cleon Gould, which Cleon inherited by will from his mother's father, Abijah Gould, 3rd. Cleon's lot extends eastward, still along Pamphylia Avenue until it joins the farm of Eugene Gould's fifty acres. This farm was left to Eugene and his sister, Mary Gould, by their father, Alfred Gould, and their mother, Mrs. Sarah Gould, still resides with them and has her widow's right in the farm. South of this farm, divided from it by Pamphylia Avenue, is the hundred-acre farm of Eli Gould (lately deceased), where reside his widow, Mary Steward Gould, her son, Edgar S. Gould, and family. This farm extends eastward along this same avenue, up to Burlington Avenue, still in ward two of Bridgeton.

The farm of Eugene and Mary Gould (these two are unmarried, brother and sister living with their mother) extends northward until it joins the seventyacre farm of George Pierce of Gouldtown (not the Salem George previously mentioned). This farm of George Pierce, which is his home farm, as he owns several, extends northward, crossing the Buckshutem road and extending to the Bridgeton and Millville turnpike, where his handsome dwelling stands; the farm also extends eastward to Burlington Avenue, which runs north and south, and to which also extends the Eli Gould farm, a half mile south. Between the Pierce farm and the Eli Gould farm is a twenty-acre lot owned by T, R. Janvier, which joins on the east end of that much of the Eugene Gould farm. East of the Eli Gould farm, from which it is separated by Burlington Avenue, is the twenty-eight-acre lot of Chaplain T. G. Steward, and eastward and northward of this lot is the more than hundred-acre farm of Rev. Theodore Gould, and his beautiful country home; this farm fronts on the Buckshutem road, there being a ten-acre lot at the northwest corner, belonging lately to Henry Dare, which separates that portion from Burlington Avenue.

Joining the northwest portion of the farm of Eugene and Mary Gould, from which it is separated by the Central Railroad, is the fourteen-acre farm and home of William Steward, which extends almost to Southeast Avenue, before mentioned, and between this and the eleven-acre lot of Cleon Gould is another eleven-acre lot owned by a lawyer. So that, as is thus shown, all this square territory lying between Southeast Avenue, Pamphylia Avenue, Burlington Avenue and the Bridgeton and Millville turnpike and trolley line, as is here indicated, as well as the farm of Rev. Theodore Gould, east of Burlington Avenue (with the exception of the lawyer's lot and the Janvier lot), is owned by the Gouldtown people, though the territory is within the limits of Bridgeton; these lands are all contiguous, divided only by roads and the Central Railroad of New Jersey.

To keep up the contiguity, on the north side of the Bridgeton and Millville turnpike, we step across this road at the northeast corner of the George Pierce seventy-acre farm where we can join the property of the estate of Francis L. Pierce, occupied by his widow and her son, and his family; this is twenty acres, off which building-lots have been sold on Burlington Avenue, which is on the west side; this property extends eastward along the turnpike until it joins the twenty-eight-acre farm belonging to Bishop B. F. Lee. Bishop Lee's property still extends eastward along the turnpike until it joins the seventy-acre Steward farm, formerly the home of James Steward, where the Steward family, whose picture is shown in this book, spent their childhood and youth. This farm, which extends on both sides of the turnpike, is now owned by Leslie S. Gould, a grandson of James Steward, the original owner.

We are now almost one and a half miles eastward from the starting point, at the west side of the home of William C. Gould, which fronts on Southeast Avenue. Going back to the Steward farm, we cross this to the south side, where we join the farm of the late Anthony Gould's heirs; it is separated by a road, running northeastwardly from the Buckshutem road, in front of Rev. Theodore Gould's residence, to the turnpike before mentioned, where it terminates at the toll gate, which is the actual beginning of the village of Gouldtown from the western direction.

The Anthony Gould farm, as well as the westerly portion of the part of the James Steward farm, joins on other lands of Bishop Lee and his three sisters — the estate of their parents. This Anthony Gould farm contains over forty acres, and extends south to the Buckshutem road. To the west of this and extending along the Buckshutem road westwardly, which divides it from the farm of Rev. Theodore Gould, is the home and twelve-acre lot of Stephen S. Steward, the carpenter and builder. South of the Anthony Gould farm and on the south side of the Buckshutem road is the farm of Milton Pierce (unmarried) comprising some thirty acres; this joins the farm of Rev. Theodore Gould, on the west, farms (two) of Lorenzo F. Gould on the south, and other farm lands of Bishop Lee and his three sisters on the east. These Lee lands also lie on both sides of the Buckshutem road, and join

A Gouldtown Woman and Her Driving Horse. Photo by Her Grandson.

on the southeast that portion of the Anthony Gould farm. To the east of the Anthony Gould farm lies the farm of William H. Gould, his son (deceased) and this joins the James Steward farm at its southeast corner, and the lands of Preston Gould, Reuben Cuff, and Frank Webster, which lie between the road which goes to the tollgate before mentioned and the turnpike.

William Gould's lands also join the lands of the estate of Pierce Gould, inherited from his father, Elisha Gould, 1st, and which are now owned by Anna Gould, granddaughter of Pierce Gould and daughter of Augustus Gould. This Pierce Gould tract extends out to and across the main road from Fairfield to Woodruff, terminating at a distance of two and a half miles from our first starting point, and all are contiguous properties; but within this large territory is a plot of fifty-two acres, belonging to the Stevenson estate, which lies between the farm of Rev. Theo. Gould on the south and the estate of Francis L. Pierce on the north, and another plot of ten acres formerly owned by Gideon Pierce, but now owned by a white man. These two plots lie between Burlington Avenue and the James Steward farm and Lee estate, on the south side of the turnpike. These two plots, comprising sixty-two acres, are entirely surrounded by the farms of George T. Pierce on the west. Rev. Theodore Gould on the south, James Steward and Lee estates on the east, and farm of Bishop Lee and Francis L. Pierce estate on the north. South of the farm of Rev. Mr. Gould are lands of the Jonathan Gould estate, Lorenzo F. Gould's farms (he also owns the farm of Jonathan Gould, his father).

From the northern point of the Steward farm, going to the southern point of the Rev. Gould farm, crossing lands of the estate of Anthony Gould and to the southern line of L. F. Gould's farms is a distance of one and a half miles. Still further south, and still contiguous, are lands of William Wilson (whose mother was a Gould) and Jacob Coombs (whose mother was a Pierce), comprising nearly one hundred acres.

To the eastward of these last tracts comes the ancient estate of Elisha Gould, 1st, which has been before alluded to, as well as lands comprising the old Gould possessions of the heirs of Abijah Gould, 1st, Samuel Gould, 1st, and Elisha Gould, 1st, as bequeathed in the ancient will of Benjamin Gould of 1777.

Cottage of Stephen S. Steward.

To the eastward and northward of these ancient estates and the ancient estates of Wanaca Pierce, 1st, and his brothers, Anthony, Menon, John, and Benjamin Pierce, are hundreds of acres, now owned by Goulds and Pierces, with now and then a Murray — the latter, however, being small possessions.

The only survivor of the family of Adrian Pierce is Steward Haines Pierce, who resides on the old homestead farm of his father at the eastern end of the settlement of Carmel. Adrian's estate was about seven hundred acres, and was divided among his heirs. Most of it has been disposed of by them, before their deaths.

From the home of William C. Gould at Bridgeton on the west to the farm of Stewart H. Pierce on the east is a distance of seven miles and a person can go from one extremity to the other and be continuously on the lands of the colored residents of Gouldtown. This immense territory, comprising over five thousand acres at the present time, is composed of both farm lands and woodlands, but the greater portion of it is woodland, and a large increase to the original holdings. The largest holders of these woodlands are William C. Gould, Albert Gould; heirs of Benjamin Gould; heirs of Holmes Pierce; George

T. Pierce; Peter Pierce; Holmes Pierce, Jr., Charles Lloyd; John Murray, 4th, heirs of Jacob Pierce, and others.

Some Leading Families and Their Line of Descent

Of the present descendants of the inhabitants of Gouldtown may be found family branches in all parts of the country from the Atlantic to the Pacific Coast.

Some of these branches, for obvious reasons founded on well-known American prejudice, will not be given here. They are white people and happy, prosperous, and some of them distinguished, and it would add nothing to the happiness or comfort of them to let their children even know of their descent. I received last week a letter from a lady in the West, the daughter of a man who was a close boyhood friend in our boyhood days, asking me if I knew her father's relatives. She had heard her father speak of me often before his death a few years ago. I had kept track of him; he was a brave soldier and a heroic officer for over three years in the Union Army in the Civil War. He was not the only one from this place (Gouldtown) whom I had known in the same capacity, who, having gone West, lost their identity of color, and become soldiers and officers in the war, and had raised honored families. Others I have known in other spheres of life as well. If their posterity can be called "deceived" I would not undeceive them.

There are two sisters, daughters of Mr. and Mrs. B. F. Pierce, the one recently residing on the Atlantic coast, at Longport, Atlantic City, the other at Tacoma, Washington. They are Miss Ethel Pierce and Mrs. Jennie Jones. They are descendants of Benjamin Gould, 2nd, on the mother's side, and Adam Pierce, the Revolutionary soldiers on their father's side.

The family of Lorenzo F. Gould is conspicuous for its general intelligence; two daughters, Miss Agnes Gould and Miss Alice Gould (now Mrs. Clifton Mosely), were schoolteachers in Atlantic and Camden Counties. Miss Lucette Pierce, niece of Mr. Gould, is principal of the Gouldtown public school and has been a teacher in Somerville, and Atlantic City, and elsewhere. They are Normal graduates. They are descendants of Benjamin Gould, 2nd, and Rev. Furman Gould, and of Anthony Pierce, 2nd.

Leslie S. Gould and Edgar E. Gould, sons of the late Eli Gould, are prominent farmers. They are descendants on their father's side from John Murray, 1st, and Elisha Gould, 1st, and on their mother's side from Benjamin Gould, 2nd. Timothy Gould and Aaron Paul Gould, farmers and truckers, are descendants on their mother's side of Wanaca Pierce, 1st, and Mary Murray, and on their father's side of Charles Gould, son of Elisha Gould, 1st.

Joseph Gould, the farmer, who resides on the homestead of his grandfather. Rev. Furman Gould, is a Gould on both sides, his mother being a daughter of Abijah Gould, 2nd. Furman and Abijah were brothers, sons of Abijah Gould, 1st. One of his grandmothers was "Kitty" Gould; the other was Rachel Hicks.

Bishop Benjamin Franklin Lee, extensively known all over the United States and in Europe, who, as well as his interesting family, has been quite distinguished, is a descendant of Benjamin Gould, 2nd, on his mother's side, and of Abel Lee, of Salem County. Bishop Lee was a member of the great Ecumenical Council which met in London a few years ago, and of other great religious bodies. Bishop Lee's mother was Sarah, daughter of Benjamin and Phoebe Gould. His only son is a distinguished student of sociology, and his daughters are accomplished teachers in Wilberforce University, of which their honored father was once president, and in which their mother, then Miss Ashe of Kentucky, was a teacher. Two of his sisters are well-known residents of Gouldtown, and the other resides in Philadelphia.

The Steward family has figured so often in this book that a mere mention is all that is here necessary., William (that is my name) is the writer; he has been engaged in newspaper work for a generation and more; he is the oldest of the brothers. Theophilus Gould Steward has been a clergyman since 1861; was first stationed in Camden, New Jersey. He graduated from an Episcopalian Theological Institute. He was sent South immediately after the close of the war to establish the African Methodist Episcopal Church where, for several years, he accomplished very successful labors. Being a French scholar he was sent to establish the African Methodist Episcopal Church in Port-au-Prince, Haiti, which he successfully accomplished. He has served most acceptably some of the largest churches of his chosen connection in the United States. He was appointed a chaplain in the regular United States army by President Harrison, the appointment coming to him unsought, and as a surprise. In this service he spent many years among the Indians on the far western frontiers. In the war with Spain he was sent to the Philippines, making several trips across the Pacific. Reaching the age limit, he was retired from the army with all the honors that go with it. He has travelled since in Mexico, and made two summer trips to England and the Continent.

Joseph Gould, son of Charles and Susan Gould, resides on the farm owned by his father. This farm came to Charles Gould in the division of the estate of his father, Rev. Furman Gould, who inherited it from his father, Abijah Gould, 1st, who inherited it from his father, the original Benjamin Gould who died in 1777. This Joseph Gould is a lineal descendant of the original Gould on both paternal and maternal sides, his mother, Susan, being daughter of Abijah Gould, 2nd, and Rachel Hicks. Joseph's wife is Almeda, granddaughter of Anthony Gould, 2nd, and Almeda Pierce.

Lorenzo F. Gould, member of the Fairfield township school-board, has Gould, Murray, and Cuff descent. His father was Jonathan Gould; his mother was a daughter of William Cuff and Prudence Murray Cuff. William Cuff was the son of Rev. Reuben Cuff and Hannah Pierce. Lorenzo F. was a soldier in the Civil War, and his son. Corporal Luther D. Gould, was a soldier in 10th United States Cavalry, and served in the War with Spain in Cuba.

Albert Gould and William C. Gould are sons of the late Furman Gould, 2nd, and Hester Cuff, daughter of the before mentioned William Cuff. There were two sisters of Albert and William Gould. One became the wife of Stephen S. Steward and is deceased, and the other, having been taken West by her uncle and aunt, grew up a white person, married and has a fine, prosperous, and intelligent family.

Frederick Gould is the last surviving member of the large family of Pierce Gould and his wife Sarah, who was a Murray; he has sons, Henry, John and Theodore, and one daughter; his wife was a daughter of John Murray, 2nd.

Frederick is now seventy-eight years of age; several years ago he was run into by a trolley car when crossing the tracks with his mule team and a load of wood. His mule team was killed, both his legs were broken, one of them in two places, and he was otherwise terribly injured. It was thought by all that he could not survive, but such was his life tenacity (characteristic of the family of his name) that he completely recovered, and had for years worked as usual. Elizabeth Lloyd, wife of Charles Lloyd, sister of Bishop Lee, is a highly intellectual woman, and though always in humble life has read more widely than many of wealth and culture.

James R. Pierce, the son of the late Ephraim and Louisa Pierce, is descended from Richard Pierce, 3rd, a son of Richard Pierce, 2nd. His wife is Isabella, another sister of Bishop Lee.

Jonathan Gould had but three children, one son, Lorenzo F. and two daughters, Hannah, widow of Rev. Jeremiah H. Pierce, of Trenton, and Annie, widow of Mordecai C. Pierce; she was Gouldtown's last postmistress. Her daughter. Miss Lucette, is principal of the Gouldtown public school.

Belford Pierce, the blacksmith, is a descendant of Anthony Pierce, 1st, and also of Anthony Gould, 2nd; his mother being Christiana, first wife of Mordecai C. Pierce. Warner K. Pierce, another member of the Fairfield School Board, is his brother.

Two brothers of Bishop Lee met accidental deaths. Both were unmarried, and both over sixty years of age. Their names were William C. and Abel. William C. left a considerable estate.

Joseph and Clarence Gould, sons of Nathan and Phoebe Gould, are full Goulds, both their parents being of that name. Nathan was the son of Abijah Gould, 2nd, and Phoebe was the daughter of Benjamin Gould, 2nd. Joseph and Clarence are both widowers.

Clarence has one daughter, Phoebe, wife of Philbert Gould, son of the late Thomas Gould, who was the son of Aaron Gould.

Preston Gould is the only son living of Anthony Gould, 2nd; he has no children.

A brother of Joseph and Clarence Gould met an accidental death when a young man by a cave-in in a sand pit on his father's farm. A sister, Nancy, wife of George Gould (nephew of Rev. Theodore Gould), resides in Atlantic City.

Besides the descendants of the original Gould, Pierce, Murray, and Cuff families residing in Gouldtown at the present time, there are numerous branches in Salem County, especially of Cuffs, and scattered in many parts of the United States and in Canada.

If the writers of this book should attempt to write to all their living relatives, they would write addresses to every State in the Union nearly, to most of the principal cities in the country and several of the larger ones in the Dominion of Canada. They would also direct to London, Liverpool, Paris, Berlin, and Antwerp.

As we now close the pages of this humble volume, we send it forth with kindly greetings to all our relatives wherever their eyes may behold it, and to our posterity that the love of the home life — the family life and all its sacred ties — the love of the old home and its traditions may be cherished and fostered, prospered and improved upon, and the sterling qualities of our forebears as we now recall them, recount, and look back upon them, may be intensified in the coming generations.

To look back for two centuries on the name which founds this community and be able to say in general terms, that it is a name unsmirched in the court annals of this county by crime, or by a drunkard or a pauper, is a heritage in which any community might rejoice, however poor it may be in material wealth.

www.ingramcontent.com/pod-product-compliance
Lightning Source LLC
LaVergne TN
LVHW091303080426
835510LV00007B/365